93105

то

1 -

THE PSALMS FOR
THE
COMMON READER

Books by Mary Ellen Chase

A GOODLY HERITAGE

MARY PETERS

SILAS CROCKETT

DAWN IN LYONESSE

WINDSWEPT

JONATHAN FISHER: MAINE PARSON

THE BIBLE AND THE COMMON READER

THE PLUM TREE

THE WHITE GATE

LIFE AND LANGUAGE IN THE OLD TESTAMENT

THE EDGE OF DARKNESS

THE LOVELY AMBITION

THE PSALMS FOR THE COMMON READER

MARY ELLEN CHASE

THE PSALMS FOR
THE
COMMON READER

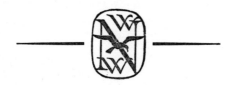

W · W · NORTON & COMPANY · INC · *New York*

Contents

Acknowledgments

Two persons have meant a great deal to me in my work on this book; I want to thank them. One is Virginia Corwin, James M. Clark Professor of Religion and Biblical Literature at Smith College; the other, Rabbi Louis Ruchames, Director of Hillel Foundation and Adviser to Jewish Students at Smith. Both know far more about the Psalms than I do; and both have been generous beyond words. They have read my manuscript, set me straight about countless things, and given me constant encouragement. I am also deeply grateful to them for their interest and friendship over many years.

M.E.C.

Foreword

THIS BOOK about the Psalms is precisely what its title says it is: a book for the common, or general reader. It is neither scholarly nor profound, in the sense of deep or extensive learning; in other words, it is not intended for the specialist in Hebrew literary studies. It is, instead, written primarily for those readers who would like to know more about the Psalms and who have found the entire collection of them as given in the Old Testament baffling and difficult, as, indeed, it is. I have tried in its pages to do what all such books are presumably designed to do: to answer questions; to explain away confusion; to suggest ways and means for more intelligent and especially for more pleasurable reading; and, perhaps above all other desires, to make old and familiar words, phrases, and lines more exciting and more real through new understanding and perception of them.

There are, of course, many books about the Psalms written by Biblical scholars from the Church Fathers in the early Christian era to men of the present time and in many countries. No subject is more fascinating or more worth further study. This brief book of mine is largely based upon their wide knowledge and research; and thanks are due from me to them all. If it results in enticing readers toward their far more valuable works, I shall be deeply gratified. If it succeeds only in making the frequent reading of the Psalms of greater value and pleasure, I shall take added delight to that which I have already had in writing it.

Mary Ellen Chase

NORTHAMPTON, MASSACHUSETTS
NOVEMBER, 1961

Explanatory Notes

1. I have purposely avoided footnotes throughout this book since they are often more distracting than illuminating, especially in an informal study of this kind. Everything of importance I have tried to include in the text itself. I have, however, prepared a list of carefully selected books which should be of great interest to my readers.

2. I have quoted throughout my book from the 1611 Authorized, or King James Version of the Psalms. There are several reasons for this choice. The Authorized Version is a work of art as well as a translation, generally accepted as one of the greatest works of art in the English language, or, indeed, in any language. In the revised versions, whether that of 1885, or the American Standard of 1901, or the Revised Standard Version of 1952, or for that matter in various other translations or paraphrases, the poetry of the Old Testament, in my opinion and in that of countless others, misses the rhythm, the stress, of the Hebrew original. Whatever may be the value of the prose of these revisions (and I do not doubt that value), their translations of the poetry surely is lacking both in appeal and in literary value when compared with that of the Authorized Version. This version has also the claim of familiarity, of centuries of usage and affection.

Roman Catholics who may read this book will find their Douay Version of 1610, either in its original form or in the eighteenth century Challoner revision, an excellent translation; and Jewish readers have, of course, their Holy Scriptures, published originally in 1917 and containing a magnificent rendering of the Psalms, many of which are practically identical with those of the Authorized Version.

The Hebrew language, unlike modern European languages, which many persons are able to read, is virtually unknown except to Biblical scholars and to fortunate Jewish people who have been trained in it either in the new State of Israel or in other lands. To the vast majority of readers of English the Psalms are actually looked upon as English poetry, as indeed they become in the Authorized Version. Regrettable as it is that they cannot be read in their original form except by comparatively few persons, it is fortunate, at least for English-speaking people, that we possess them in so beautiful and, on the whole, so accurate a translation.

3. In the Supplement at the close of this book the reader will find, for his convenience, certain psalms grouped under those types especially considered in this study.

4. I have taken pains to include also in the Supplement a brief account of Hebrew history. Some knowledge of the actual events in the history of Israel is indispensable to any understanding of the Psalms. These events reflect the times in which the Psalms were written, in so far as those times are known, and also the long background from which they come; they reflect, too, the character of the Hebrew people to whom we are forever indebted for their literature. Readers who do not know those historical events or the ancient traditions behind and within them will do well to have these securely in mind before beginning to read this book. I suggest, therefore, a careful reading, or even *study* of this historical account; and I would advise such a study before the book itself is read.

PART ONE

What Are the Psalms?

1

Their Origin and Authorship

WHEN I was a child in a small village on the coast of Maine at the turn of the present century, the Psalms played an important part in my life, not only in church on Sunday, but at home and in school. In church we heard them read; in Sunday School we were required to memorize the more familiar ones; at home their phrases were household words; and in our country school we began each day by reciting either the 23rd, or the 19th, or the 121st, or the 100th, which commanded us all to "make a joyful noise unto the Lord," even though we were all longing to make that noise elsewhere, with the Lord, I am afraid, well out of the picture.

At home my father with the help and inspiration of Psalm 91 aptly characterized a great-aunt of ours, whom none of us much liked. When we heard that she was coming for dinner with us, he defined her as "the destruction that wasteth at noonday"; and whenever she stayed for a night, she became "the pestilence that walketh in darkness." Although my mother was given to reproaching him for his employment of such holy words, we children delighted in them.

He also made use of the Psalms as a means of increasing our pocket money. Whenever we summoned up courage to tell him that our allowance of twenty-five cents a month, per child, was far too small, indeed impossible for our needs, he always informed us that we could increase it by memorizing any psalm of our choice and repeating it *verbatim* to my mother and him. Both of them during these ordeals sat with their eyes firmly fixed on the Bible, since they did not entirely trust their own long memories. Ten cents was the reward for a perfect recital; but a child received nothing if he, or she, made the slightest slip or even hesitated unduly. I can remember standing in terror before them and saying, "The Lord is my light and my salvation," praying desperately meanwhile that He would prove to be both! I earned a good many dimes in this way and early increased my knowledge of the Psalms.

In those faraway days we took it for granted, of course, that David himself had written all the Psalms; and in this assumption our parents agreed, as did practically everyone else in the Bible-reading world of their day. We used to love to repeat, strictly among ourselves, a careless and rather ribald rhyme, which our elders deplored as blasphemous, though they had at that time no reason to think it untrue so far as the authorship of the Psalms was concerned. It went like this:

King Solomon and King David lived very wicked lives,
With half a hundred concubines and quite too many wives.
But when old age came creeping on, they both were filled with
     qualms,
So Solomon wrote the Proverbs, and David wrote the Psalms.

I have since learned that this delightful verse has other variants than merely its English form. The Austrian composer, Haydn, quotes in his Journal a most pleasing German version of it; and I am told that children of yet other tongues have repeated it, probably with the same reckless abandon which we used to enjoy. I remember that I always pictured David either as a shepherd boy, blowing on some sort of pipe or flute, or as a king, clad in royal purple and twanging a full-sized golden harp, as, inspired by God, he composed the Psalms.

In the late nineteenth century certain scholars of Hebrew, largely in Germany, discovered through their linguistic and historical researches on the Old Testament that David could not have been the author of the Psalms. This doubt had been, in fact, expressed by Jewish commentators as early as the Middle Ages. He may have known, it is true, certain portions of some of the oldest among them, such as, for example, the stirring lines in Psalm 24:

> *Lift up your heads, O ye gates!*
> *And be ye lifted up, ye everlasting doors!*
> *And the King of glory shall come in.*
>
> *Who is this King of glory?*
> *The Lord of hosts, He is the King of glory.*

There is a persistent tradition that this psalm might well have been sung, at least in part, when the Ark of the Tabernacle was carried in triumphal procession from the homes of two men called Abinadab and Obededom, who had been guarding it, as we read in the 6th chapter of II Samuel, to the shrine prepared for it in David's new city of Jerusalem;

or perhaps, instead, that it was sung when the sacred Ark was brought to Solomon's Temple some fifty years later. Another tenacious tradition claims that the psalm was recited or sung in the Second Temple on the first day of the week; and in the Greek Old Testament, translated from the Hebrew in Alexandria around 250 B.C. and known as the Septuagint, this use of it is explicitly stated in its superscription, or heading.

Surely there is no reliable proof that David did not know this psalm, or, indeed, that he may not have had some part in its composition, just as there is no proof that certain psalms, or at least portions of them, were not written in his time, which we can place around 1000 B.C., or even by him himself. The considered opinion, however, of the best scholars is that most psalms, in whole or in part, were written at a far later date, that is, between 500 and 200 B.C., after the Hebrew exiles had returned to Judea in 536 or 537 B.C. from their fifty years' captivity in Babylon. Among the reasons for this opinion are (1) the lack of any exact knowledge concerning liturgical worship in the Old, or Solomon's Temple, built in the tenth century, B.C.; (2) the fact that many psalms contain references to happenings during those later centuries following the Exile; and (3) the added fact that, in general, their language would surely seem to indicate composition at a later period.

The title of the Psalms, that is *The Psalms of David*, lies deep in Hebrew tradition. Seventy-two psalms are definitely ascribed to David in their superscriptions, even to concrete events in his life; and, as we know, the writers of the New Testament Gospels as well as St. Paul in his letters assumed David's authorship of them. We cannot know how early David's name became attached to the collection as a whole.

Probably the honour of the title was accorded him because of his eminence in Old Testament history and story as a musician and as a poet, and because of the tradition which credits him with overseeing the singing in the public worship of his people, a tradition strengthened by various references to him in the Old Testament whether as the "sweet psalmist" or as the organizer of choirs.

A similar accordance of a title was given to King Solomon when the book, *The Proverbs of Solomon*, was named after him, without doubt because of his reputation, hardly substantiated by his reign, as being the wisest among men. He was, as all must know, in no sense the author of the collection, which was completed at least five hundred years after his time and which represents the maxims and aphorisms of centuries of Hebrew life and also of other and older civilizations, although he may well have sponsored the scribes who preserved the early proverbial wisdom. Nor was he the author of the so-called Song of Solomon, which is rightly called the *Song of Songs*.

We shall be, then, on far safer ground if we think of the Psalms as a collection of 150 religious songs and hymns written by several, if not by many unknown authors and extending over a period of several centuries. Some of them, or at least parts of some of them, may have been composed at a very early date in the long history of Israel. The great majority, however, were probably written after the building of the Second Temple, which was completed around 516 B.C. and which most certainly used the singing of psalms as a part of its various liturgies. We are not even sure when the collection or compilation of the Psalms as we know them was made, but doubtless some time after the year 200 B.C., or at least during the course of that second century, perhaps even as late as 100 B.C.

The fascinating and now familiar discoveries of those ancient manuscripts known as the Dead Sea Scrolls, discoveries made in caves near the Dead Sea between the years 1947 and 1956, have already contributed knowledge about the Psalms. These ancient manuscripts, inscribed on papyrus, leather, or copper, and many of them of the Old Testament books, were copied by the members of a religious community, probably the Essenes, who had a monastic establishment at a place known as Qumran in the arid wilderness on the northwest shore of the Dead Sea. Just when they lived their communal life at Qumran cannot be given in exact dates, but probably from around 100 B.C. to 70 A.D. It is not inconceivable, however, that they may have lived elsewhere at some earlier time.

That they were devout men, dedicated to the Jewish Law and bent on reading and preserving their Holy Scriptures, is evident from the wealth of copying done by their scribes. From complete scrolls and from thousands of fragments discovered in the caves, in which they were hidden probably because of an attack by the Romans, who after 63 B.C. became the rulers of Israel, we know that the Psalms ranked, with Deuteronomy and Isaiah, among the Old Testament books which they held of greatest value. They surely copied and recopied the Psalms many times; and it is interesting to note that in several of their copies they were aware of the poetic form and separated the lines of the verses, in other words, wrote the poetry *as* poetry.

Their love and veneration for the Psalms is not only important in itself, but is also helpful in determining at least approximately the time of the collection and compilation of the Psalms as one Old Testament book. Since the Qumran scribes not merely copied, but also made comments on certain psalms and since in at least one Qumran manuscript the Psalms are, on the whole, in the same order and with the same titles as in the later extant Hebrew Scriptures, it would seem safe to assume that the Psalms as a book had already been collected and established as Holy Scripture. For this reason our date, given as sometime after 200 B.C., is probably not too far from correct.

These Essenes, or these dedicated Jews living at Qumran, whatever name they possessed, also wrote Thanksgiving Psalms of their own, which, although they show both in their expressions and ideas the influence of Biblical psalms, exhibit a new type of composition, and also later religious and literary development. If, as seems most likely, these hymns of their own were composed during their life at Qumran, we have another good reason for thinking that our book of the Old Testament Psalms was earlier and already a valuable possession in their library, even although the actual manuscript (or manuscripts) from which they copied has not, so far as we know, survived.

As all careful readers of the Old Testament realize, there are other poems, some of them surely more ancient than our Psalms, scattered throughout its books. For example, there is the song attributed to Miriam, the sister of Moses, who, we read in Exodus 15, "took a timbrel in her hand" and accompanied by women "with timbrels and with dances," sang:

Sing ye to the Lord, for he hath triumphed gloriously!
The horse and his rider hath he thrown into the sea.

There is the battle song of Deborah in the 5th chapter of Judges, one of the oldest and most famous of war poems, or hymns of victory, which was certainly familiar to the writer of Psalm 68, since he quotes from it. There is the song ascribed to Moses in Deuteronomy 32; and in I Samuel 2 the thanksgiving Song of Hannah for her long-awaited son, Samuel. There are the two magnificent poems about Wisdom, one in Proverbs 8:22–31, the other, Job 28, both psalms and both perhaps contemporary in composition with certain of those in our Old Testament book. Many of the exalted poems of the Second Isaiah, who lived in Babylon with the exiles in the middle of the sixth century, B.C., and most of whose work is contained in Isaiah 40 to 55, are psalms in the best sense of that word, as are also many passages in the book of Jeremiah, the prophet, who lived and exhorted his erring people around 600 B.C. and who surely influenced both by his thought and language the writing of later psalms.

In the New Testament, St. Luke in his Gospel writes, or re-phrases, or repeats three songs: the *Magnificat* of Mary, which resembles in many ways the song of Hannah; the *Benedictus* of Zacharias, the father of John, the Baptist; and the *Nunc Dimittis* of old Simeon in the Temple of Jerusalem. All these, both in the Old Testament and the New, are in form, material, and manner of utterance quite as truly psalms as are those in the Psalter.

Nor must we think of the Psalms as only an Hebraic form of poetry. Such poems and hymns were common also to other ancient peoples, such as the Assyrians, the Babylonians, and the Egyptians. Most reliable and learned Biblical scholars have discovered from excavations of clay tablets in Syria and from the careful deciphering of them that the Canaanites, from whom, as we know, the Israelites wrested their Promised Land, also wrote and presumably sang their

psalms to their gods, the Baals, and that certain of these
Canaanitish hymns suggest adaptations and borrowings by
later Hebrew poets from this older literature of their neighbours.

It is difficult, if not impossible to say to what extent this
more ancient poetry influenced the Hebrew psalmists, although it is probable that certain of these poems, or portions
of them, were known among the more educated people of
early Israel. Their small land was on the highway of travel
between Egypt and the great Eastern empires of Assyria
and Babylonia; it had known both Assyrian conquest and
many years of Babylonian overlordship; and nothing could
be more likely than that they should garner from their conquerors, or from friendly and literate traders, or perhaps
from travel of their own, at least something from the literature to the south and east of them as well as from that of
the former possessors of their country, the Canaanites.

Scholars of Egyptian, Assyrian, and Babylonian religious
literature have become convinced that several of these
ancient hymns, whether they were written in praise of the
Egyptian sun-god, or of the Assyrian moon-god, or of the
Babylonian goddess Ishtar, have a basic relationship to our
Hebrew psalms. Not only is their construction similar, as
we shall see later, but in the case of Egyptian and Babylonian hymns there are phrases, idioms, even ideas common
to all. Both the poets of Babylon and those of Israel would
make their enemies their "footstool"; write of their gods, or
God, as "standing at their right hand"; compare their salvation to a "lamp" or a "light"; say that their "tears" have
been their "meat and drink"; lament that they must "go
down to the pit," and cry out, "How long, O Lord, wilt
thou be angry?" Both the poet of Psalm 104 and the mono-

theistic king, Amenophis IV, or Ikhnaton, of Egypt, who came to power around 1375 B.C. and who is accredited with a "Hymn to the Sun" as the source of life, write of the dawn and the twilight, of the daily labour of men, of the lions that come forth from their dens, of the fish in the sea, of the "manifold works of the Creator," and of the fact that man lives only through his dependence upon God. Are these common themes characteristic only of two monotheistic poets? Or did the author of Psalm 104 know Ikhnaton's hymn? Since it was written while some of the Hebrew tribes or families were still in bondage in Egypt, in the century before the Exodus, is it even possible that some knowledge or memory of it might have survived among them as a people and been handed down to their descendants? Or could it have come to them by way of nearby Phoenicia, which during the time of Ikhnaton was a province of Egypt?

In spite of the researches of dedicated scholars, such questions will probably never be truly or even satisfactorily answered. They lie buried too deeply in the long past. Meanwhile the Psalms remain, far more beautiful in literary expression than the hymns which have preceded them or perhaps, directly or indirectly, influenced them; far more exalted in their conceptions of God; far more dignified and noble in their desires and hopes for men. They have been for centuries and still remain the priceless legacy to countless millions, both of Jewish and of Christian peoples, and, indeed, to those who claim no clearly defined religious faith.

Many Biblical students and scholars are quite contented to call the Psalms "The Hymnal of the Second Temple," that is, of the Jewish sanctuary built after the return from the Exile in Babylon upon the ruins of the Temple of Solomon. They give the book this title because they are convinced that most of the 150 psalms were sung by choirs in religious services. I have always thought the title at best incomplete, and even inappropriate. Many psalms in the collection are quite clearly not designed for any ritual purpose, but are instead purely individual expressions of profound feeling and intended for private meditation and for personal devotions rather than for public worship. I like better, in common with several of the best scholars, to think of the Psalter as an anthology of religious poetry, prepared and published for the sake of satisfying and nourishing the minds and hearts of many people, whether in the Temple, or at home, or about their work.

I have always thought, too, that John Calvin in his *Commentary on the Psalms*, written in 1563, has given the best description of them. He says: "I may truly call this book an anatomy of all parts of the soul, for no one can feel a movement of the Spirit which is not reflected in this mirror. All the sorrows, troubles, fears, doubts, hopes, pains, perplexities, stormy outbreaks by which the hearts of men are tossed, have been depicted here to the very life."

His words are true, and I believe that they give us the best description ever written of the Psalms. They are truly a mirror, and not only of one people, but of all mankind; for they reflect in their words and images both those highest reaches of which the soul is capable and also the more inglorious qualities of human nature. The poets of the Psalms write of the loneliness of the human spirit which no earthly comfort can heal; the solitude of mental pain; black hours of despair; the waves and the billows upon which all men and women are tossed. Yet they write as well of the wonder of life itself; of the glory of creation; of the incomparable gifts of God; and of His constant care for His children. They hate as well as love, curse as well as praise, pray for revenge as well as for mercy.

Let us think of the Psalms, then, as the spiritual epic of an ancient people, and not alone of one people or of one time, but of all people and of all time. Only in reading them in this way can we ever come to understand and truly to value them.

2

Their Collection and Use

MANY READERS of the Psalms do not realize that our familiar Psalter, our collection of 150 psalms, is really an assembling of five separate collections, of five smaller psalters. If one looks carefully, however, at the close of certain psalms, specifically Psalms 41, 72, 89, 106, and 150, one will easily discover that this is surely true. Each of these numbered psalms, except 150, ends with a brief doxology; in the case of 150, the entire psalm is a doxology and obviously intended to conclude the book as a whole. *Blessed be the Lord God of Israel from everlasting, and to everlasting. Amen, and Amen,* writes the poet of Psalm 41. *The prayers of David the son of Jesse are ended,* says the author of Psalm 72. And the inspired poet of Psalm 150 in his six verses, or stanzas, closes the completed collection by enumerating the places and the reasons for praise of God and even the musical instruments to be used in that praise. Indeed, one might truly say that Psalms 146 to 150, inclusive, all form a part of this mighty, exultant doxology; and so similar are these five psalms in their language, their

contents, and their style that one is almost compelled to believe that all were composed by the same poet, whether he
was "the psalmist" or "the prophet" of their superscriptions.

There is another fact which points conclusively to the
gathering together at different times of these separate collections. This is the occurrence of the same psalms in the
anthologies of individual editors or compilers. As one learns
upon examination of the psalms in question, Psalm 14 in the
first book is almost identical with Psalm 53 in the second.
Several verses of Psalm 40 are repeated in Psalm 70. Psalm
108 is a combination of verses from Psalms 57 and 60. This
repetition surely suggests that a favourite psalm was preserved by more than one collector; in other words, that the
editor of one anthology either liked a certain psalm so much
or knew it to be so generally popular that he did not hesitate
to repeat it, even although it had already been included in
other collections. There is, of course, always the possibility
that he did not know of this inclusion at the time he made
his own anthology. For we cannot be sure when the separate
books were gathered together, just as we cannot be entirely
sure that the five books were first published separately, one
at a time and probably over a period of two centuries at
least, although the evidence clearly points to this procedure.

The first two books are ascribed to David and usually
known as the *Davidic Psalms*, although in the second book,
that is, Psalms 42 to 72, there are several psalms not directly
accorded to him or to concrete events in his life. The three
books following are not so specifically ascribed, although
the doxologies at their conclusions bear strong witness to
them as independent collections. Some psalms in these books
are still called psalms of David; others in their superscriptions would seem to have been written for guilds of singers

such as the Sons of Korah, presumably a choir, or for Asaph, perhaps a "chief musician," as he is sometimes called, or a choir leader. The unknown author, or scribe, of the two books of Chronicles, who probably lived and wrote around the third century, B.C., lists by name in one of his chapters many of these Temple singers. According to him, Asaph was a "seer" of David's time; but we cannot safely place too much confidence in this statement. Other psalms in these three books are known as Hallelujah Psalms because they are calls to praise and would seem to imply congregational singing; still others are called Songs of Degrees, or Ascents, and were presumably sung by pilgrims on their way to special festivals or High Holidays in Jerusalem. And there are several others, such as the beautiful Psalms 90 and 91, which, in spite of their superscriptions, are clearly songs of individuals voicing their faith in God and their perception both of His power and of His mercy "in all generations."

It is impossible to be certain of the full meaning of some of the superscriptions. Perhaps, as in Psalms 57, 58, 59, and 75, the Hebrew word *al-taschith*, or "destroy it not," may refer to some measure which was popular at the time and to which the hymn is to be sung; or, as in Psalm 22, to a tune known in Hebrew as "the hind of the morning." Other words clearly refer to the accompaniment by musical instruments, whether to strings, to instruments of percussion, or to horns and trumpets. The word *Selah*, which is used seventy-one times throughout the Psalter, has puzzled scholars for centuries. No one is sure what it means or what its presence indicates. Perhaps a pause? Perhaps a repetition? Perhaps something quite different.

As we have already learned, not all psalms were written for Temple worship, but since many of them were, it is interesting to know, so far as is possible, something about how they were probably sung, upon what occasions, and to the accompaniment of what ancient musical instruments. It is probable that psalms used in worship in the Second Temple (completed as we have already seen around 516 B.C.) were sung antiphonally or responsively, the tenors singing one verse, the basses another. There were doubtless, as well, boy sopranos and altos in the largest and best of the choirs. Perhaps women, too, were sometimes numbered among the singers. At all events, Psalm 68 describes a procession which included "damsels playing with timbrels."

In certain psalms there are refrains as in Psalm 107:

> *Oh that men would praise the Lord for his goodness,*
> *And for his wonderful works to the children of men!*

This refrain occurs four times in the psalm and was doubtless sung by the choirs in chorus, or perhaps by the entire congregation.

Not only does the Chronicler write of the singing of psalms in the Temple and even quote from those sung, such as from Psalms 96 and 105, but the Hebrew superscription for Psalm 92 states that it is a "song for the Sabbath." The Greek Old Testament, the Septuagint, is even more explicit in its headings to the Psalms, clearly naming those to be sung on the several days of the week. As to the great Hebrew religious festivals at which psalms were certainly sung or chanted, there were three observed during the time when the greater part of the Psalter was being written in its five collections and later compiled as one book.

There was, first of all, the spring Feast of the Passover, which commemorated deliverance from Egyptian bondage and which more than any other observance meant the very root of Israelite religion, indeed the very life of Israel as a people. In the summer at the beginning of the barley harvest there was the Feast of Weeks, or Pentecost. In the autumn the Feast of Tabernacles, or of Booths, took place, called by the Hebrews *Succoth* (their word for booths), or the Gathering-in. This feast, which came at the time of the Jewish New Year and which lasted for seven days, was one especially dear to the hearts of the people. It is described in the book of Deuteronomy as a time of rejoicing for all members of every family. Surely it was an occasion of song and revelry, perhaps not unlike our own Thanksgiving. Families who found the journey possible flocked to Jerusalem from near and far, on asses, on camels, or on foot, taking pride in living in hastily erected "booths" or in tents (the real meaning of *tabernacles*) after the manner of their nomadic forefathers in the desert after their escape from Egypt. This feast is the one which St. John records in the seventh chapter of his Gospel when Jesus went up "in secret" to the Temple, and "on the last and great day" of the celebration as well as in "the midst of the feast" spoke to the many people gathered there.

It is difficult to be entirely precise and exact as to ancient Hebrew musical instruments. Many of these, to be sure, are mentioned in various books of the Old Testament as well as in the Psalms; yet we have today small means of knowing just what they looked like. Some, however, are portrayed on Egyptian and Assyrian reliefs and other monuments, as well as on Jewish coins. And we must always remember that the predominant element of all music in ancient Israel was rhythm, not harmony, and that melody as we know it today held a very subordinate place.

Probably the most primitive musical instrument was the

timbrel, the Hebrew *toph*. This, we remember, was used by Miriam and the dancing women with her, as she sang her ancient song; and in the tragic story of Jephthah's daughter in Judges 11 we are told that this unsuspecting girl came out to greet her father "with timbrels." We remember, too, those women in I Samuel 18 who welcomed King Saul from his return from the wars with the Philistines and who aroused jealousy in the king by striking on their timbrels (here called *tabrets*) and singing:

> *Saul has slain his thousands,*
> *And David his ten thousands.*

A timbrel was a ring of wood or of metal, covered with a tightly drawn skin. Sometimes it had pieces of metal around its rim, like a tambourine. Its great age is attested by representations of it on Egyptian seals almost as early as 3000 B.C. It is mentioned four times in the Psalms.

Another percussion instrument, cymbals, though named only once in the Psalms, is frequently referred to in other Old Testament books as being used by choirs of Levites, who seem to have been among the chief Temple singers, and by the "sons of Asaph," as well as by David himself. There were apparently two different kinds of cymbals, the "loud" and the "high sounding," both of which the writer of Psalm 150 names in his list of instruments for the praise of God. The loud cymbals when struck together must have made a harsh, brazen clang, whereas the high sounding ones were far more musical.

Horns or trumpets were certainly used in religious worship. There were evidently several kinds of these wind instruments, and some of them date back to very early times if we can trust to persistent tradition. The most ancient was doubtless the *shophar*, or the ram's horn trumpet, which was perhaps not so much used for making music as for giving signals or announcing great events, such as the outbreak of war or the coronation of a king. In the book of Joshua we are told that the walls of Jericho fell down when seven priests blowing on seven ram's horns had marched for seven days around that city. The ram's horn trumpet is still sounded today in Jewish temples and synagogues on the New Year Festival and at the close of the Day of Atonement. Other trumpets, probably of silver, were apparently used in religious services, perhaps for a kind of fanfare. In Numbers 10, two of these are made by Moses at God's command; and he, also, is supposed to sound them at times of alarm or for purposes of assembling the people. He is expressly told, however, that the trumpets are to be blown as well "in solemn days" and over "burnt offerings" and "peace offerings." Still other trumpets were smaller, perhaps about a foot and a half in length with a bell-like mouth not unlike our cornets. Indeed, the word *cornet* is used with *trumpets* in Psalm 98.

As to a more simple sort of wind instrument, there was certainly the pipe, in Hebrew the *chalil*, which means *reed*. Perhaps oddly, it is not mentioned in the Psalms; but it is spoken of at least ten times in other Old Testament books. In ancient Greece shepherds played on pipes as we know from Classical literature; and they may well have done so in ancient Israel. Probably the pipe was similar to a flute or to an oboe; and perhaps the word extended even to crudely constructed whistles made of pierced wood and blown upon by country boys and girls.

Stringed instruments are mentioned frequently in the Psalms,—harps, and psalteries, and that baffling, lovely "in-

strument of ten strings," which the poets of Psalms 33, 92,
and 144 so carefully designate. Does it simply describe the
harp as having ten strings, or was it a special sort of harp?
This seems impossible to discover. We can perhaps only be
sure that the usual harp of the Old Testament was in no sense
like our large orchestral harps of today, but, rather, a kind
of lyre, the strings of which were stretched across a sounding board, made of cypress or perhaps of sandalwood, and
which was small enough to be easily carried about. David's
harp, called *kinnor* in Hebrew, was probably such a lyre,
played either with the fingers of the right hand or with a
plectrum. The psaltery, which is not called *kinnor*, but has
a name of its own, *nebel*, may have been a somewhat
larger harp. Some scholars particularly interested in ancient
Hebrew musical instruments think that the psaltery re-
sembled a zither; others compare it to a lute or to a
dulcimer. Certain early Jewish coins picture a U-shaped
harp or lyre, the very presence of which on coins might
well suggest its popularity.

The harp in its various shapes and forms has caused more
confusion and aroused more questions than has any other
musical instrument recorded in the Old Testament. It surely
holds first place in the Psalms and was clearly the favourite
of the men who wrote them. Indeed, our book itself, which
takes its English title from the Greek word *psalmos*, means
literally "to play upon a stringed instrument," or, interpreted more freely, "songs sung to the accompaniment of a
stringed instrument." In the Hebrew Scriptures its title is
Tehillîm, which means simply *praises*.

The Psalms, as we read in the Gospels and in the book of
the Acts, were known and quoted in the earliest years of the
Christian era. St. Paul in his letters to the first churches

urges the singing of "psalms and hymns." They were surely used in the earliest medieval monastic orders of which we have record, read, chanted, or sung by monks and by nuns as daily offices, or "hours." Since that day they have been an inherent part in the services of all Christian sects, whether Catholic or Protestant, just as they have been and still are the constant inspiration of all forms of Jewish worship from its distant beginnings even until now.

The very mystery of their origin perhaps makes them of greater richness and value. Since we do not know their authors or their exact dates, they become in a peculiar and intimate sense the expression and, indeed, the possession of all men. Conceived as many, if not most of them were in a time of doubt and despair, of subjection and oppression, by a noble people whose actual existence as a race was threatened, they, more than any other religious poetry, speak to the human heart. That their poets, even in tears and sorrow, could sing of their invulnerable faith in the God of their fathers, has brought light into many a darkness, lent horizons of new hope to men and to nations alike. In their candid, realistic searchings into life, their understanding of its bitterness as well as of its solace, its eternal, unanswered questions as well as its assurances, they might have been echoing the words attributed to Heraclitus, that Greek philosopher who lived not long before their own time: *God is winter and summer, war and peace, light and darkness, bread and hunger.*

3

Their Various Types

THE PSALMS are far more clearly understood and will be vastly more appreciated if one lifts them from their five collections and reassembles them as types, according to their various forms and subjects. Then they fall into some reasonable or at least perceptible sort of order, which is denied them in their Old Testament book, and can be read and studied *as* types just as we study different kinds of English poetry, whether narrative in ballad form, or lyric in many molds, or blank verse. It is, of course, true that Hebrew poetry is far less flexible as to form, being governed by one predominant arrangement in lines and verses; and yet it has a wide variety of subjects.

Some forty years ago a German scholar named Hermann Gunkel, who published his first important work on the Psalms in 1926, became aware of the helpfulness of such a classification and proceeded to make one. In his *Gattungen*, or *types*, he discerns these several differing forms and subjects: hymns, laments, thanksgivings, royal psalms, wisdom psalms, pilgrim songs, and other minor types. His careful and even minute classification has deservedly met with a wider acceptance than has that of any other scholar, although several before his day had recognized that the Psalter contains a great variety of poems. Gunkel's full number of types is far too large to be considered, one by one, in this brief book, his complete classification much too elaborate. Also, as he himself realized, the composition of certain psalms, or, perhaps more accurately, the final compiling of them, contains elements of more than one type, or character, a fact suggesting that they are not always unities in the strict sense of that word, but sometimes combinations.

I have thought it best in my book to present only a few of these types, those which I consider the most clearly identifiable and also the most interesting for readers of the Psalms. In general I have followed Gunkel's classification; but I have included in my own smaller list only those psalms best known and those which I believe, with some necessary exceptions, to be of the highest literary excellence,—in other words, those which deserve most careful reading and study. For it is obvious that no reader can possibly become fully familiar with all the 150 in the Psalter; and it is also undeniably true, as I shall try to show, that many in the entire collection are inferior to others in literary expression and value.

In my own classification I have sometimes departed from Gunkel and other scholars simply because certain psalms seem to me to be of a different nature and to belong in another division. I may, of course, be wrong; but, like most persons, I find it difficult to abandon my own ideas even for those of readers far more learned than I, especially since no exact proof is available as to who is right. My own divisions, each of which I shall try to explain and justify, are the following: (1) hymns (2) thanksgivings (3) laments (4) historical psalms (5) psalms about Nature (6) pilgrim songs and (7) psalms of personal meditation and reflection. These seven types seem to me both to include the best psalms and also to be illustrative of the Psalter as a whole.

Hymns

Although, as I have said, "The Hymnal of the Second Temple" seems unsatisfactory as a title for the Psalms on the ground that many were surely not written for choir or congregational singing, there are others which were clearly composed and arranged for that purpose. And among these are some of the most beautiful in the Psalter.

In general those psalms which are hymns are more objective in character than are several of the other types which we shall study. They were written for the public praise of God; and in them He and His works are glorified. Man, his sorrows, his doubts, his problems, even his experiences are in these hymns subordinated to the worship of the Almighty, the Lord of hosts, and the King of kings. Even prayer gives place to praise.

The most characteristic hymns usually begin with an *introduction* in which the psalmist calls upon the assembled people to join in this praise of God. Two excellent examples of such an introduction are the opening verses of Psalms 95 and 103. In Psalm 95:

> *O come, let us sing unto the Lord!*
> *Let us make a joyful noise to the rock of our salvation.*
> *Let us come before his presence with thanksgiving,*
> *And make a joyful noise unto him with psalms.*

In Psalm 103:

> *Bless the Lord, O my soul,*
> *And all that is within me, bless his holy name!*
> *Bless the Lord, O my soul,*
> *And forget not all his benefits.*

Other hymns, such as Psalms 146 and 150, begin merely with *Praise ye the Lord;* and several, like Psalm 106, add the stirring words, *For he is good; for his mercy endureth forever.* Psalm 117, the shortest of all psalms, indeed the shortest chapter in the entire Bible, illustrates perfectly in its entirety the introductions to the longer hymns of praise:

> *O praise the Lord, all ye nations!*
> *Praise him, all ye people!*
> *For his merciful kindness is great toward us,*
> *And the truth of the Lord endureth for ever*
> *Praise ye the Lord!*

The *main portion* of the hymn following the introduction deals practically always with those things for which God is worthy to be praised. These verses may tell of God's attributes, His righteousness, His mercy and lovingkindness, His justice, the demands He makes of men; or they may describe His wondrous works in His creation of the world; or His tender care for all His children. Certain psalms, such as Psalm 97, would seem to have been composed for His coronation or His enthronement in the Temple and suggest His final power "above all gods." Sometimes, as in Psalm 107, a *refrain* is used. In this long and beautiful hymn God's care and providence over all manner of persons are extolled: over those who travel, over prisoners and captives, over the sick, over the sailors, over the farmers. After each is described, in his wayfaring, his sufferings, his afflictions, his dangers, his labours, the refrain occurs:

O that men would praise the Lord for his goodness,
And for his wonderful works to the children of men!

There is also a secondary refrain in this psalm, preceding the chief one, although its words are not always identical in its four appearances:

Then, they cried unto the Lord in their trouble,
And he delivered them out of their distresses.

Finally, many hymns have *conclusions* which are apt to repeat the introductions or at least to echo them in slightly different words. The conclusion to Psalm 8 repeats the identical words of the introduction, *O Lord, our Lord, how excellent is thy name in all the earth!* The final verses of Psalm 103 echo and enlarge upon its initial command, *Bless the Lord.*

Such hymns, as we have seen in an earlier chapter, were doubtless sung at all the great festivals of the year, at the Passover, the Feast of Weeks, and the Feast of Tabernacles, which last feast coincided with the New Year, when after a long season of drought the first welcome autumn rains were longed for; and since ancient Israel was a people endowed not only by distinctive poetic gifts, but by a sense of drama as well, we may be sure that the singing of them held a prominent place in public worship. Various references in the Old Testament as well as in certain psalms themselves, such as Psalm 68, make us sure that the singers moved in processionals, that there were "players on instruments" of every sort used at the time, that, in short, the rites and ceremonies were moving and impressive.

After more than two thousand years and with the lack of entirely reliable records, we cannot be sure of what actually occurred in the Temple when these hymns were sung, what sacrifices were offered, what singing and even sacred dances took place; and it would be only confusing to become enmeshed in the conflicting theories of scholars concerned in such matters. It is far better for the general reader of the Psalms to know the hymns themselves in all their dignity and glory. There is, however, in the Apocryphal book of Ecclesiasticus, written probably in the second century B.C., around the year 180, a description of such ceremonial and pageantry which gives us at least some picture of what must have taken place at that time in a service led by "Simon, the high priest," a man whom the author of Ecclesiasticus describes "as the morning star in the midst of a cloud, and as the moon at the full":

*Then shouted all the sons of Aaron, and sounded the silver
    trumpets,*
*And made a great noise to be heard, for a remembrance before
    the Most High.*
Then all the people together hasted,
And fell down to the earth upon their faces
To worship their Lord God Almighty, the Most High.
The singers also sang praises with their voices,
*With great variety of sounds was there made sweet mel-
    ody. . . .*
Till the solemnity of the Lord was ended;
And they had finished his service.

Thanksgivings

The line between hymns and thanksgiving psalms is without doubt a faint one, not easily discerned. Nevertheless, in my own reading and study I have found it helpful, since, although many thanksgiving psalms were doubtless sung in public worship, others clearly express the gratitude of the individual and his own understanding of the gifts and mercies of God in his own particular life. When the poet of Psalm 30 ends his song by saying that he will give thanks to God forever, for he knows that joy must come to him in the morning even after a night of weeping; when the unknown author of Psalm 34 says that God has delivered him from all his fears, and not only him but a "poor man" whom he knows; when he who wrote Psalm 116 thanks God for saving his soul from death, his eyes from tears, and his feet from falling—all these men are uttering their own personal words of gratitude. So is the author of at least the first part of Psalm 40, which by the almost universal agreement of scholars is really two independent poems. This man has "waited patiently for the Lord"; but now his feet are brought up "out of the miry clay" and set "upon a rock." In his mouth is "a new song." He knows with humility and awe that he can never "reckon up" the "wonderful works" which God has done for him.

Like the hymns, the thanksgiving psalms usually begin with an exultant *introduction:*

> *I will bless the Lord at all times.*
> *His praise shall continually be in my mouth.*

Or:

I love the Lord
Because he hath heard my voice.

There usually follows the *narration* or the vivid description of the psalmist's trouble: a serious illness, a dearth of faith, the slander of his enemies, poverty, or perhaps mental pain and despair; and after this there ensues the marvellous fact of God's deliverance. In several of the thanksgivings as in the hymns the *conclusion* is similar to, or sometimes identical with, the *introduction*. Psalm 118, for example, one of the best of the thanksgiving psalms in its joy and exultation, begins and concludes with the familiar

O give thanks unto the Lord, for he is good,
For his mercy endureth for ever.

Of all the psalms of thanksgiving Psalm 139 in my opinion holds first place. It is, in fact, from any point of view, one of the finest psalms in the Psalter; many readers will, perhaps, accord it the highest place. It might well be considered a psalm of meditation and reflection; yet gratitude is its theme throughout and gratitude combined with an overwhelming sense of wonder. Its poet in his grateful surprise over his very creation is like Thomas Traherne crying in his ecstasy:

How like an Angel came I down!
How bright are all things here!
When first among His works I did appear,
O how their glory did me crown!

There is throughout this psalm a touching simplicity, naïve and childlike in its ingenuousness. Its writer cannot for a moment forget or even entirely realize that God has searched him and known him, his "downsitting" and his "uprising," all his ways. Such knowledge, he says, is "too wonderful" for him, too high, too impossible of attainment. Even his nights shine as the day. He not only praises God because he is "fearfully and wonderfully made," but he begs God to search him for sinful thoughts, for to him in his joy and wonder any sinful thought on his part is utterly at variance with the amazing goodness of God. He is even so overcome by gratitude and incredulity that he hates all the enemies of God, all wicked men who take God's name in vain. Perhaps among all the writers of the Psalms this man is the most human and appealing. His very effervescence is intoxicating; and we wish it had been our good fortune to have known him, wherever he lived, whoever he was.

These thanksgiving psalms, of which there are some twenty in the Psalter, besides the constant echoes of thanksgiving in many more, perhaps beyond any other type cast over the entire collection its atmosphere of exultance, its beautiful sense of amazement and wonder. In their frank, if unwilling acceptance of the eternal problem of pain and suffering, in their renewed hope and buoyancy, they bring simple and nameless men of all generations out of the past into the present and thus become not for an age but for all time.

Laments

As John Calvin has already told us, the Psalms are a mirror reflecting all the emotions of the human soul. We must, therefore, expect to find within them laments for trouble and sorrow, outcries against the slings and the arrows of life. Moreover, since most of them were written during years of subjection when the very existence of a people was threatened, and since the Hebrews were among all peoples perhaps the most intense and even violent in their emotions, laments were as natural to them as were rejoicings. There were surely many bitter hours in their long experience when to rejoice was impossible. They had known invasion, destruction, and death, and the lesser misfortunes of drought, famine, poverty, and plague. Small wonder, then, that their poets cry out again and again against all that causes them anguish and despair: their enemies who at least *seem* to be blessed by God; their loss of hope and, worse still, of faith; illness, and their fear and hatred of death; the awful absence of God in their thoughts.

Sometimes the lament is one not of an individual, but rather of an entire people, the subject nation of Israel. Such is Psalm 44 in which the writer vividly contrasts the mercies of God toward His people in the past with His apparent neglect of them in the present. Once He delivered them out of bondage and saved them from their enemies. Now He has put them to shame, scattered them among the heathen, made them objects of scorn and derision to their unwelcome neighbours, bowed their souls to the dust.

Such national laments were without doubt often connected with ritual fasts or with elaborate Temple ceremonies, designed for seasons of penitence and prayer on the part of the people. This we gather from references in the Old Testament which record proclamations for fasts or for solemn assemblies. Even the very form of the lament may well have been traditional or, perhaps, conventional. Certain scholars note that laments were composed and sung by other peoples in the Near and Middle East, such as the Babylonians, the Canaanites, and the Assyrians, in their attempts to propitiate their gods or to bring about their favour. We know that definite forms of expression and behaviour were expected from professional mourners and from early bands of so-called "prophets." But since the details of such ceremonies, or even the proof of them, are impossible to ascertain today with any degree of accuracy, we shall be far more wise simply to read and study the lament as a type of psalm which still holds meaning and value for us after many centuries.

Two characteristic expressions of national laments are the words *Why* and *How long*, which echo the bewilderment and the impatient endurance of a whole people. The writer of Psalm 10 cries:

> *Why standest thou afar off, O Lord?*
> *Why hidest thou thyself in times of trouble?*

And Psalm 80 is filled with the broken questions of the poet on behalf of his people:

> *O Lord God of hosts,*
> *How long wilt thou be angry*
> *Against the prayer of thy people?*

Such questioning is echoed in other national laments, such as Psalms 44, 74, and 79.

More plentiful and far more interesting among the laments are the outcries of individuals, of human souls in torment. Gunkel claims that such laments are far more numerous than any other type of psalm. This is doubtless true; and yet it is significant that there is rarely a lament which before its close does not express hope and confidence with that almost incredible resilience of the Hebrew mind and heart. Men may be cast down, but they are not defeated; forsaken and yet not deserted; plunged into darkness, yet still able to see light. And it is unquestionably because of this deathless hope that, in spite of the number of psalms of distress, they do not take from the Psalter its prevailing atmosphere of faith and trust.

The lament as a type usually begins with a *call for help*, as in Psalm 6, which is clearly the psalm of someone very ill:

> *O Lord rebuke me not in thine anger,*
> *Neither chasten me in thy hot displeasure.*
> *Have mercy upon me, O Lord; for I am weak.*
> *O Lord, heal me; for my bones are vexed.*

Sometimes this complaining call is lost in an almost angry cry as in the familiar opening words of Psalm 22:

> *My God, my God, why hast thou forsaken me?*

Again, as in Psalm 130, the psalmist's cry, although less personal and more universal in his acceptance of life, is equally one of despair:

> *Out of the depths have I cried unto thee, O Lord.*

In most psalms of this type the opening cry is enlarged upon by a *description of the complaint*. Psalm 22 is again an admirable example. Its writer sees himself despised by men; laughed to scorn because of his faith in God; encompassed by enemies; "poured out like water." His "bones are out of joint"; his heart is "like wax"; his "tongue cleaveth" to his jaws; he is brought "into the dust of death."

The complaint is often followed, though sometimes preceded, by a *petition*, often pathetic in its despair:

Be not thou far from me, O Lord!
O my strength, haste thee to help me!

And few laments close without a *vow* of continued faith and confidence, of determination to persevere, whatever the cost.

Through many years of reading books and studying commentaries on the Psalms I have found few students and scholars who share my enthusiasm for Psalm 102, perhaps I should say my delight in it, for to me it is charming and even amusing. Surely no other lament is so frank and unabashed in its list of grievances! Those more learned than I are concerned with whether it was originally one psalm, or two, or even three, and with whether it is a national rather than a personal lament. I am, instead, concerned and touched by the psalm itself, especially by its first twelve verses. Its description in these verses of a despondent, sick, and deserted man brings to my mind similar hours in my own life and banishes all questions of mere scholarship. This poor soul is apparently all alone on the top of his house, with no one coming to see him. Perhaps they are staying away because they are, quite reasonably, tired of his groanings! He describes himself as a "pelican of the wilderness," as "an owl of the desert." He has a high fever; he cannot eat. He is terribly afraid lest he be taken away "in the midst" of his days by that God who "shalt endure forever!" I am sure with the scholars that many of his utterances are noble and even holy and that the latter half of his psalm may well represent his nation rather than himself; but it is his wretched and vividly described plight which interests me and which makes me smile even in the midst of his terrible distress.

Psalms 42 and 43, now generally conceded to have been originally one psalm instead of two by reason of their similar language and of their identical final verses, form perhaps the most moving of all the laments. Its author is so concrete and simple in the anguished questions which he asks of God that we find our concern with his sorrows easy and inevitable. He says at the opening of his poem, in a comparison deep in the beginnings of his nomadic race, that his soul panteth after God "as the hart panteth after the water brooks." He, too, had gone to the house of God with all his friends and neighbours for some holy day, some festival; and yet all the joy and praise there had not sufficed to keep him from his misery and despair. He recalls the history of his people, and in spite of his tears and sorrow, which taunt him day and night with doubt, he still clings to God's light and truth and knows that they will, perhaps at long length, lead him again to the tabernacle and to the holy hill.

Once is not enough for his questioning, his doubt, and his hope. Three times he asks his bewildered questions, and three times he gives sure and certain proof of his tortured, yet undying faith:

> *Why art thou cast down, O my soul?*
> *And why art disquieted within me?*
> *Hope thou in God; for I shall yet praise him*
> *Who is the health of my countenance, and my God.*

Historical Psalms

The God of the Old Testament is primarily the God of its history. He possesses many other attributes, as we shall see in a later chapter of this book; but, first and foremost, He is the Lord God of the people of Israel and of their history from the beginning. He has made Himself known to them as their God through the performance of specific acts and in the occurrence of particular, concrete events. The Old Testament throughout bears witness to these acts and these events, directly in its historical books, indirectly in its prophecy and poetry. It recounts them, commands in its Law that they shall never be forgotten. This conviction, indeed this knowledge to the Hebrew mind, that God has chosen Israel to be the people through whom He is to make known His purposes for mankind, is so basic that no understanding of the Old Testament is possible unless this conviction, this faith is clearly understood. When the poet of Psalm 103 writes,

> He made known his ways unto Moses,
> His acts unto the children of Israel,

he is giving expression to the assurance which lay deepest in every Hebrew heart.

It is but natural, then, that psalms should be written both to extoll this conception of God and to relate His mighty acts for His people. In many psalms, not as a whole given to God's work as the Lord of history, there occur verses or stanzas in which this work is praised; in others the material is largely if not wholly concerned with these God-controlled historical events. Sometimes these historical psalms, which perhaps as a group lack the literary excellence of other types, are relatively general in character; sometimes they are concrete and explicit.

Psalm 46, which opens with the familiar words,

> *God is our refuge and strength,*
> *A very present help in trouble;*

Psalm 145, which speaks throughout of God's mighty acts and wondrous works; Psalm 114, in which not once, but twice, during the wanderings of the Children of Israel,

> *The mountains skipped like rams,*
> *And the little hills like lambs;*

—all these are examples of God's concern for His people from their bondage in Egypt, throughout the years of their pilgrimage and their conquest of Canaan, the founding of their kingdom, its conquest by great empires, their exile, and their return home. All alike tell of the everlasting glory of His sovereignty, the imperishable strength of His dominion and power. They do not, however, record His specific acts as do Psalms 78, 105, 106, and 136.

In Psalm 78, which with its seventy-two verses is the longest in the Psalter (except for Psalm 119, really an exercise in Hebrew acrostics) the writer warns at the outset that he is about to relate God's wonderful works which all have heard from "our fathers." This he proceeds to do, in somewhat stilted and prosy words, from an early rebellion of "the children of Ephraim" to the "marvellous things" done in the land of Egypt; from manna and quails in the wilderness to the days of King David himself. The writers of Psalms 105 and 106 emulate his good, or bad, example, the first going back even to the patriarchal ages of Abraham, Isaac, and Jacob, and the second recounting a dozen events, wicked and wondrous alike, from Aaron's golden calf and Moses' disobedience, to the unfailing patience and forbearance of God during all these many years.

The author of Psalm 136 is perhaps the most explicit of all, although his brevity is commendable in view of Psalm 78! His concrete canticle must have been sung on some festival occasion since each of its twenty-six verses closes with the refrain:

For his mercy endureth for ever.

He is not content to begin his psalm with freedom from Egyptian bondage. He goes back to the Creation itself, extolling the sun, the moon, and the stars. After the Red Sea and Pharaoh have been dealt with, he recalls the famous and terrifying kings whom God has vanquished for Israel, Sihon, king of the Amorites, and Og, king of Bashan. And although, like the author of Psalm 78, he cannot claim high distinction as a poet, he is surely untiring as an historian and a chronicler.

One psalm which is based on the history of Israel uses a single period or even episode as its subject. This is Psalm 137, the most beautiful of the historical psalms. Most scholars see it not as an historical psalm, but instead as a lament, at least in its first four verses, as indeed it is; most of them, too, deplore its succeeding five verses in which the psalmist cries bitter curses upon the enemies of Israel, especially upon Babylon, the place of captivity and exile. I myself have always looked upon it as belonging among the historical psalms, as written by someone who perhaps either actually recalled the Exile itself or to whom it has never ceased to be real because of the experience of his fore-fathers; and I am quite willing to condone and even to understand his rage and his longing for revenge against the enemies of his people. Among all the poets of the Psalter not one excels him in his command of language or in his portrayal of human sorrow, which is as evident in the fall of his words as in the images which fill his mind. And the haunting question which he asks at the conclusion of his vivid picture of those in exile might well be the question of all his race throughout its sad and turbulent history:

By the rivers of Babylon, there we sat down,
Yea, we wept, when we remembered Zion.
We hanged our harps upon the willows in the midst thereof.
For there they that carried us away captive required of us a
*   song;*
And they that wasted us required of us mirth, saying:
Sing us one of the songs of Zion!
How shall we sing the Lord's song in a strange land?

Psalms about Nature

Most readers of the Old Testament are, I feel sure, in-clined to think that there is in its pages far more poetry written about nature, her manifold aspects and ways, than there actually is. They remember, of course, the magnifi-cent 38th and 39th chapters of Job; the beautiful passages in Isaiah, particularly the writings of Isaiah of Babylon, the poet as well as the prophet, who, as we have seen, is often called Second Isaiah; or perhaps various descriptions in Jeremiah of birds, the stork, the partridge, and the swal-low, which he obviously knew and loved. In the Psalms they recall "green pastures" and "still waters," and the declaration of the heavens to "the glory of God." Nevertheless, in spite of all these and of countless interspersed passages throughout the prophetic and poetic books extolling God as the creator of the world and its riches, there is actually among all the books of the Old Testament comparatively little of such poetry; and this fact is especially true of the Psalms.

The psalmists glorify God, to be sure, as the sovereign power over a vast and miraculous world; they consider His heavens, His moon and His stars; and yet all these wonders are always seen by them not as glories in themselves, but rather as further manifestations of His righteousness and His providence toward mankind. Except for many passages here and there throughout the Psalter, such as the triumphal lists given in Psalms 146 to 150 of all the wonders which fulfill His word—mountains and hills, cedars, snow and hoarfrost, clouds and stormy winds—there are but three psalms given entirely or at least largely to His praise as the Creator of a cosmic universe. These are Psalms 19, 29, and 104. Each is distinctive; and each is a great literary achievement.

Since we shall in a later chapter make a special study of Psalm 19 as perhaps the truest portrait of the Hebrew mind in terms of its thought, its sense of dedication and obligation, and its tenacious faith, I shall here call attention only to its first six verses, which clearly form a hymn of praise to God, the Creator, His heavens, His days and nights which constantly utter His glory throughout all the earth, and, above all else, His sun,

Which is as a bridegroom coming out of his chamber,
And rejoiceth as a strong man to run a race.

Psalm 29, which is too little known and appreciated by most readers of the Psalms, pictures in a most graphic way a thunderstorm from the time of its rising over the Mediterranean along the coastal mountain range to its final dying away in the wilderness of the south. Few psalms are so vivid in their imagery. The poet, after his call to worship and to praise, repeats again and again "the voice of the Lord" (in Hebrew *qôl Yahweh*), his words for the thunder. This voice is upon the western waters; it peals over the summits of the mountains; it breaks the cedars, even the mighty cedars of Lebanon, which skip like a calf or like a unicorn before the high wind; it shakes the wilderness; it "maketh the hinds to calve" before their time because of their terror; it is punctuated by flashes of lightning, "the flames of fire," which light up all the forests. And as the rain follows, the poet is apparently reminded of the story of that ancient flood which once covered the earth at the command of God.

Some scholars believe that the literary roots of this psalm lie deep in archaic pagan liturgies, perhaps in those of the Phoenicians. Whatever its origins, it remains one of the masterpieces of the Psalter; and it should be read often for pure pleasure.

Psalm 104, which has been mentioned in an earlier chapter as perhaps influenced by a much older Egyptian hymn to the sun, is justly admired for its description in full detail of all the manifestations of God's power in His creation of the universe. The poet here carefully forms his psalm into clearly designated parts or sections, all of much the same length. He wants neither to omit any miracle of God's "manifold works" nor to extoll one above another. His order, it is interesting to note, is similar to that of the story of the Creation in the first chapter of Genesis. The sky, the earth, and the waters receive his initial praise; but he is not in the least unaware of smaller matters. Much of the charm of his poem, in fact, lies in his naïve gratitude for the simpler, more tangible blessings of life:

> *He causeth the grass to grow for the cattle,*
> *And herb for the service of man,*
> *That he may bring forth food out of the earth;*
> *And wine that maketh glad the heart of man,*
> *And oil to make his face to shine,*
> *And bread which strengtheneth man's heart.*

He seems to enjoy recording his own knowledge of the countryside and of its pleasures:

> *The trees of the Lord are full of sap;*
> *The cedars of Lebanon which he hath planted,*
> *Where the birds make their nests.*
> *As for the stork, the fir trees are her house;*
> *The high hills are a refuge for the wild goats,*
> *And the rocks for the conies.*

Even the "beasts of the forest" are less terrifying to him since they, too, "seek their meat from God"; and the "great and wide sea," always a source of awe and of fear to a hill people, yields him wonder because of the ships upon it and the "small and great beasts" within it. There is even wry humour in his reference to leviathan, the great sea monster —the whale or the crocodile, perhaps?—whom God has made for Himself as a plaything!

All in all, he is one of the most appealing of the psalmists as he declares in his conclusion that, in spite of earthquakes and volcanoes, too, he "will sing unto the Lord" as long as he lives on this various and beautiful earth. For he, like his God in Genesis 1, has looked carefully upon it and found it "very good."

Pilgrim Songs

No other type of psalm, especially in terms of human significance, rivals or perhaps equals in appeal that type known as the pilgrim song. As its title suggests, it was a psalm sung by those who had journeyed from their homes, sometimes in distant places, to Jerusalem for one or more of the great festivals of the year.

That such pilgrimages were customarily made we know both from commands concerning them in the books of Exodus and Deuteronomy and from stories of the journeys themselves. In the first and second chapters of I Samuel there is an account of a very ancient pilgrimage made to the sacred shrine at Shiloh, before the building of the first, or Solomon's Temple, by a man named Elkanah, who went every year with his family to worship and to sacrifice. Again, the story of Joseph and Mary in St. Luke's Gospel, when they lost Jesus, "supposing him to have been in the company" among "kinsfolk and acquaintance," is another narrative of a return journey from the Feast of the Passover in the spring, a pilgrimage which took place a thousand years after that of Elkanah and his household.

Such pilgrimages had, of course, other features and aspects than those purely religious. They were, without doubt, the dreams of excited children for months before entire families set forth with friends and neighbours, mules and asses, bags and baskets of provender, sheep and lambs

for sacrifice, and, as well, harvest offerings from storehouses
and fields. Here was the one chance during the year to see
new or perhaps old faces, to exchange tidings, to indulge in
talk and story-telling around campfires, and to enjoy, as
on all such journeys, the sights and the sounds of an unfamiliar countryside. And whenever houseworn and tired
women who longed for a change of scene felt obliged to
give up the coveted outing, as did Hannah, the beloved of
Elkanah's two wives, who forfeited her pilgrimage to stay
at home with her baby, it must have seemed a sacrifice
indeed!

Not all the excitements were pleasurable ones. There
were dangers as well on such journeys, as the writers of the
pilgrim songs affirm. There were the blazing desert sun by
day, sand-storms, and hot, searing winds. There was peril
from roving bands of robbers who might well invade the
night encampments, always guarded by sentries; there were
possible wild beasts, illness, plagues from insects. There
were the old to care for and children to be watched over
and tended. There was always the weariness of long days
spent in plodding forward, since most of the pilgrims
marched on bare or on scantily-sandalled feet, the asses and
the mules being used largely for the necessary provisions,
or for the aged and the very young.

Without doubt all these features of the journey, both
perilous and pleasurable, account for the concrete and vivid
imagery in many of these songs:

The sun shall not smite thee by day,
Nor the moon by night.

If it had not been the Lord who was on our side
When men rose up against us;

Then they had swallowed us up quick,
When their wrath was kindled against us.

Behold how good and pleasant it is
For brethren to dwell together in unity!

The Lord shall preserve thy going-out and thy coming-in
From this time forth, and even for evermore.

The sight of the Holy City upon its hills was, of course, the thrilling climax to all such pilgrimages. Roads from literally every direction were so much lower than the citadel itself that it was always visible on its height at the end of the journey. When they first saw its buildings against the sky, its walls, and, above all, its Temple, the pilgrims burst forth exultantly:

I will lift up mine eyes unto the hills!

They sing, too, in these songs about Jerusalem itself, the goal and the end of their journeying, a goal both sacred and tangible, both visible, yet in its deepest sense invisible:

Our feet shall stand within thy gates, O Jerusalem!
Jerusalem is builded as a city that is compact together;
Whither the tribes go up, the tribes of the Lord,
Unto the testimony of Israel,
To give thanks unto the name of the Lord.

And again:

They that trust in the Lord shall be as Mount Zion,
Which cannot be removed, but abideth for ever.
As the mountains are round about Jerusalem,

So the Lord is round about his people
From henceforth, even for ever.

And yet again, in glad and grateful remembrance:

When the Lord turned again the captivity of Zion,
We were like them that dream.
Then was our mouth filled with laughter,
And our tongue with singing.

All these lines, many of them, of course, familiar to most readers, come from Psalms 120–134, a group known by their common superscriptions and, better still, by study and research, as Songs of Degrees, or Songs of Ascent, or Songs of Pilgrimage. These fifteen psalms, nearly all of which contain some proof of their identity as pilgrim songs, may, it is thought by some scholars, once have been a single small collection. Most of them are short psalms, and practically all of them contain references both to pilgrimages and to singing in chorus. It is very likely that such groups of pilgrims, like those recorded by the author of Nehemiah when he writes about the Return from the Exile in Babylon, brought with them "singing men and singing women," who would lead the services surely held along the way upon the Sabbath and doubtless upon other days as well.

My own favourite among the pilgrim songs is Psalm 84, not contained among the fifteen acknowledged to belong to this type. It is but fair to say that certain scholars do not classify Psalm 84 as a pilgrim song at all. Nevertheless, Gunkel does; and his authority is helpful, especially since we owe to him our classification into types. Surely it has all the qualities of a wayfaring hymn; and I cannot bear to look upon it as anything else.

Its very first verse suggests a band of tired, footsore, eager men, women, and children, gazing upward toward the Temple and, now forgetful of all their hardships, crying:

How amiable are thy tabernacles, O Lord of hosts!

They have evidently had a long and difficult journey, passing through arid valleys which, by the mercy of God, have finally been visited by welcome rain; but their strength has not failed them, only increased. Here they are, at long last! And as they gaze upward toward the Temple, they watch with new wonder the birds who dare to make their nests even among those sacred stones:

Yea, the sparrow hath found a house,
And the swallow a nest for herself where she may lay her
young!
Even thine altars, O Lord of hosts, my King and my God.

Perhaps no single image throughout the Psalms is so real, alive, and moving as is the sight of those birds, fluttering in and out among the parapets and towers, busy, confident, at home. They are no longer "fowls of the air," that over-all term for many birds throughout the Old Testament, but, instead, the common, familiar sparrows and swallows, known to all.

Nor does any other pilgrim song express the unified ecstasy of this one from its first to its final verse. Joy, surprise, excitement, wonder, trust, and faith—all are here—and all are uttered in such fresh and frank language that the psalm holds a high place among the 150 in the entire collection. Even if it were not sung by pilgrims who at last look upon their "amiable" Holy City—and I devoutly believe that it was!—it remains a treasure for all pilgrims who must today trudge through their own Valleys of Sorrow and who long also to "go from strength to strength."

Psalms of Personal Meditation and Reflection

Among the 150 psalms there are many which, obviously not designed for public worship, can best be called psalms of thought, of reflection, of meditation. These psalms or poems were clearly written by men who longed to express their own ideas, to make use of their own imaginations. It is hardly necessary to say that in this type of psalm, as of course in all literary productions, there is a wide divergence in the value of the ideas, in the range and character of the imagination, in the power and felicity of expression. Some among these meditative psalms are, in comparison with others, relatively mediocre pieces of work; perhaps their more personal nature is bound to reveal more clearly their value as literature. There are four, however, which through the centuries since they were written have been justly renowned both for their material and for the perfection and beauty of their form and language. These are Psalms 23, 27, 90, and 91.

All these great poems profit in many ways by the very absence of those devices which were needed for choral singing: the ringing summons to praise; the repetition of words and phrases; the use of the refrain. They profit, too, by the absence of any more or less prescribed order of arrangement. Their authors, freed from rules or conventions, could concentrate on their own thoughts and perceptions; on their understanding of the ways of men and of life itself; and, above all else, on the nature and purpose of God as their own minds grasped that nature and those purposes. They were not philosophers, for the Hebrew mind, in general, was not philosophical, at least in the speculative sense; but they were surely sensitive men of dreams and visions and of long and deep thoughts about life as they knew it. Since their poems were composed to be read rather than sung, they could give expression to their own conceptions in their own way; seek out images, metaphors, symbols which would best convey these innermost conceptions; use language in the noblest manner possible to them. All these things they have done, and so carefully and well that their psalms are without doubt, together with Psalm 139, which we have already considered as a thanksgiving psalm, among the most finished and perfect in the entire Psalter.

Although these four psalms differ widely in their subject matter and in their means of expression, they have certain qualities in common. All are carefully formed; none is deficient in structure, or in the unity of its final effect. All are vivid in their imagery, whether this imagery deals with *shepherds and sheep, a host of enemies, secret places, the snare of the fowler, shadows, the transitory nature of grass, the eternity of time.* All deal in symbols, those visible signs of the invisible. All show a flexible command of language; a variety of sentence arrangement; and a steady progress toward the development of the poet's thought. And, finally, all in varying degrees express faith in God, not merely as the God of the fathers or even as the daily "sun and shield" of men, but as that continuing Power which "throughout all generations" and "from everlasting to everlasting" sustains not only men, but all mankind in its earthly pilgrimage.

Surely the best known and probably the best loved of

these four psalms is Psalm 23. Except for the Lord's Prayer, the Beatitudes and the Ten Commandments, this Twenty-third Psalm is better known than any other complete passage in the Bible as a whole. It has been repeated for centuries by countless millions and without doubt deserves all the affection accorded it.

Its appeal, aside from the permanent appeal of the known and the familiar, lies, of course, in the perfection of its simplicity, the universal nature of its need. The metaphor which gives it much of its meaning lies deep in the history of an ancient race. Its imagery, if not profound or varied, is clear, quiet, and satisfying; and, although the range of its thought and expression is limited when compared to the greater psalms of its type, its very universality confers upon it an objective quality which, in itself, it hardly deserves.

Psalm 27 is really a finer piece of work, stronger, far more vigorous both in its wealth of imagery and in its marked variety of expression. There is nothing mannered or studied about this psalm. Its author does not care for "still waters"; he suggests a gushing torrent. Perhaps the chief value of his psalm lies in its singular force and directness, its fervid, unhalting pronouncements. There is not a verse within it which does not possess this sheer strength of utterance whether its writer asks questions, or bursts into exclamations, voices imperatives, or declares realities. One has the feeling that he resents the lack of other constructions by means of which he might be even more generous in his outpourings! Surely no other psalm, from its perfectly balanced assertions and questions at the beginning,

The Lord is my light and my salvation; whom shall I fear?
The Lord is the strength of my life: of whom shall I be afraid?

to its sure and certain commands at the close, lends such a sense of complete and abounding vitality. The very prodigality of its utterance as well as of its assurance is a battle cry against the forces of inertia and apathy.

This psalmist is the St. Paul of the Old Testament, glorying in his afflictions as St. Paul glorified, in his letters to Corinth and to Rome. His enemies, the loss of his father and mother, a host of other evils including even war—all these become as nothing when seen in the light of his invulnerable, pulsating, almost rampant faith. The virtue of his impassioned writing is that it convinces his readers, at least for the time being, both through the brilliance of its variety and the force of its expression. His job, as he obviously conceives it, is to banish doubt and indifference, to insure their death through his outbursts of life. The Psalter owes him a great debt and not alone for his faith, but for his sense of craftsmanship as well.

Nevertheless, with all their appeal and unquestionable value, neither of these psalms equals or even approaches in value Psalms 90 and 91. In these two psalms the dignity and the glory of the Psalter are established in terms of human thought, perception, compassion, and understanding. Each is concerned not only with man, but with all mankind, not only with the individual in his "threescore years and ten," but with all who live, have lived, or will live on this earth. The countless centuries of man's experience and of man's fate fill the minds of these two poets; the ceaseless ebb and flow of life; the slow struggle of the human spirit toward that Wisdom which is not only God's, but God Himself. To them it is He who is our "dwelling-place," who alone can deliver us from terror and destruction, in whose "secret

place" and under whose shadow we can fulfill, even im-
perfectly, our destinies.

> *Lord, thou hast been our dwelling place in all generations,*
> *Before the mountains were brought forth,*
> *Or ever thou hadst formed the earth and the world,*
> *Even from everlasting to everlasting, thou art God.*

Both these unknown poets are masters of imagery and of
metaphor. In Psalm 90:

> *For a thousand years in thy sight*
> *Are but yesterday when it is past*
> *And as a watch in the night.*

In Psalm 91:

> *He shall cover thee with his feathers,*
> *And under his wings shall thou trust.*
> *His truth shall be thy shield and buckler.*

Both understand the beauty, the dignity, and the inspiration
of language at its noblest. And, perhaps above all other
qualities, both are able to lose themselves, their personal
anxieties and concerns, in the common fears, the common
hopes, and the common needs of men in all ages. Nor does
either forget the eternal value of the individual, even the
work of his hands, and the constant strength given him by
the hands of the angels of God.

In view of the height, depth, and breadth of these psalms
and of the power of their writers to put their visions into
words, the superscriptions of both, doubtless attached to
them, later by some editor or compiler, are inappropriate, if

not a trifle absurd. Psalm 90 is called "a prayer of Moses," a title probably used as a tribute to the greatest man of ancient Israel, the bulwark and, indeed, the founder of its faith. Psalm 91 is most incompletely described as "the state of the godly." Such titles mean little and can well be set aside as misleading and unsatisfactory.

If a distinction must be made between these two master-pieces of the Psalter, Psalm 90 is as poetry superior to Psalm 91. Its language is more varied and powerful, its subject more universal. Yet both record the highest and deepest religious conceptions and convictions. They would have delighted the prophet Amos, who, probably three centuries earlier, astounded his listeners at Bethel by declaring that all men of whatever race or colour are the children of God:

> *Are ye not as children of the Ethiopians unto me,*
> *O children of Israel? saith the Lord.*
> *Have I not brought up Israel out of the land of Egypt?*
> *And the Philistines from Caphtor?*
> *And the Syrians from Kir?*

And they would likewise have given assurance to Isaiah of Babylon in his teaching that the God of Israel is the Lord of all:

> *Before me there was no God formed,*
> *Neither shall there be after me.*
> *I, even I, am the Lord,*
> *And beside me there is no saviour.*

These poets of Psalms 90 and 91 are concerned neither with outcries nor laments, neither with personal sin nor suffering and the problems which they inevitably present at all times and to all thoughtful minds. Convinced that God alone is the end of all man's searching, that His mystery from the beginning is as profound as is His grace, they reflect upon that mystery and that grace, asking only that His power, care, and glory shall never be forgotten by His servants and by their children throughout all generations.

PART TWO

How Should the Psalms Be Read?

1

Their Poetic Structure

HEBREW poets knew nothing of rhyme in our sense of that word; nor did they use meter as we know it in various forms of English poetry. But although rhyme was non-existent to them, they did employ a clearly recognizable rhythm which was really metrical since it was based on accented words, that is, on a measured beat of long and short syllables. Several scholars have attempted, not too successfully, to describe this meter by determining how many accents or stresses appear in a given line of Hebrew poetry; but since in so many psalms, as elsewhere throughout Old Testament poetry, these lines are various and inconsistent in their number of accented words, there are obviously no hard and fast rules which can be either generally or safely applied. It is far wiser, I think, to understand the poetic structure as a whole without attempting to apply rules which are in many cases unworkable. It is true that there are often, if not usually, *three* stresses to a line, that is, three words which receive the beat, or accent; but so many and differing mixtures occur that no safe and sure pattern is conclusive.

The basic literary feature in the Psalms as in all other Hebrew poetry is *repetition*. Their poets in the excess of their feeling want to drive home a truth—a conviction or an assurance, a grievance, a hope, or a joy, a curse or a blessing, a call to praise or a lament. To them, once is not enough. They must say twice what they long to say, or three times, or even four in a succession of often tumultuous lines. They may and usually do employ different words; yet the meaning of the lines is the same as is clearly evident in those that follow:

Bless the Lord, O my soul!
And all that is within me, bless his holy name!
Bless the Lord, O my soul,
And forget not all his benefits:
Who forgiveth all thine iniquities,
Who healeth all thy diseases;
Who redeemeth thy life from destruction;
Who crowneth thee with lovingkindness and tender mercies.

Or again:

O give thanks unto the Lord!
Call upon his name!
Make known his deeds among the people.
Sing unto him, sing psalms unto him!
Talk ye of all his wondrous works.

This repetition of ideas in successive poetic lines or units of thought has been known since the mid-eighteenth century as *parallelism*. Nor was this parallelism peculiar only to the Hebrew poets. It appears also in Egyptian, Assyrian, Canaanite, and Babylonian poetry and was, in fact,

obviously common to the ancient literature of the Near and
Middle Eastern peoples.

The term *parallelism* was given it by an English scholar
named Robert Lowth, who noted that the lines in all
Hebrew poetry were so closely related one to another that
one was, in fact, *parallel* to the other, dependent upon the
other for its full and completed meaning. In other words,
he recognized as a fundamental principle that every verse
must consist of at least two lines and that the second line
must in some more or less definite way complete, or satisfy
the expectation or the curiosity aroused by the first.

Lowth recognized and named three outstanding types of
this parallelism: *synonymous*, *antithetic*, and *synthetic*. In
synonymous parallelism, which is by far the most frequently
used type in the Psalms, the second line merely repeats the
thought of the first; in *antithetic* parallelism, the second line
represents an antithesis to the first; in *synthetic* parallelism,
the second line supplements or completes the first by giving
some consequence or result of the first and in this way
synthesizes, or joins, the thought of each. Since Lowth's
time other varieties of parallelism have been discerned by
various scholars and critics; but most of these, with the
exception of *climactic* parallelism, are only minor variations
of the three kinds named by him.

In the hands and minds of gifted poets this form of writing, which may well seem stilted, can be extremely varied.
Lines can be shortened or lengthened, increased in number
or inverted in form; rhythms can be quickened or slowed
down; pictorial images can be employed and sharp contrasts
drawn; and every manner of sentence structure can be
brought into use. One has but to read the ancient Song of
Deborah in Judges 5, a song composed around 1125 B.C.,

to become aware of this variety at its very best. Nor is it lacking in the Psalms, most of which were written centuries later. We have already become familiar with Psalm 27, an excellent example of this wealth of literary expression. Psalm 68, although not nearly so distinguished a poem, illustrates admirably in its far greater length the diversity of construction possible to parallelism. One might well think that any form of poetry, seemingly so rigid in its basic structure, would prove inflexible, that its writers might well be impeded or hampered by its formal requirements; yet the very opposite is made evident in the Psalter as a whole. Some psalms are, of course, more rich and various than others; but the verse form alone surely raised no barriers to the Hebrew poetic genius.

And now for a clearer understanding of the poetry itself in its various forms of parallelism:

As we have seen, the rhythm depends entirely upon the *accent,* or the *stress* upon the words in the line, which is usually called a *stich.* Two of these lines form, of course, a *distich,* or a *verse,* although the verses by no means always consist of only two lines. The parallelism in each verse may well extend to three or even to four lines. Two lines are, however, the most common verse form.

The *stanza,* sometimes called a *strophe,* is a subject of much disagreement among those who would critically analyze Hebrew poetry. Sometimes it is formed by a single verse; at other times, as in Psalm 104, it clearly includes several verses. There seems to be no convincing evidence that the psalmists consciously used stanzas. Their division is dependent more upon the content of the psalm than upon its form. For example, in Psalms 112 and 114, as in many others, stanzas exist largely as single verses, whereas in Psalm 107 the stanzas are long and separated from one another by a refrain, as is true also in Psalm 42–43.

There are countless verses in the Psalter written in *synonymous* parallelism:

Hear this, all ye people!
Give ear, all ye inhabitants of the world!

The heavens declare the glory of God;
And the firmament showeth his handiwork.

Thou shalt tread upon the lion and adder;
The young lion and the dragon shalt thou trample under feet.

The righteous shall flourish like the palm tree;
He shall grow like a cedar in Lebanon.

The second form of parallelism most commonly used in the Psalms is *synthetic*. Several, if not many scholars contend that, strictly speaking, this form is not parallelism at all, since the lines are clearly not parallel in actual structure and meaning. Yet the construction is so often used throughout the Psalms that it seems best not to argue here about its endurable name, but rather to recognize its frequent presence. Its order is sometimes variable, the consequence, or occasion, or exemplification occurring in the first line instead of in the second. The form most often employed, however, is the direct one where the cause or consequence follows the act or the thought:

I cried unto the Lord with my voice,
And he heard me out of his holy hill.

Or:

> *The earth is the Lord's, and the fullness thereof,*
> *The world, and they that dwell therein.*
> *For he hath founded it upon the seas*
> *And established it upon the floods.*

Yet sometimes the consequence or the cause is inverted as in Psalm 122:

> *I was glad when they said unto me,*
> *Let us go into the house of the Lord.*

And in Psalm 91:

> *Because he hath set his love upon me,*
> *Therefore will I deliver him.*

Frequently in like manner the occasion precedes the result as in Psalm 8:

> *When I consider thy heavens, the work of thy fingers,*
> *The moon and the stars which thou hast ordained;*
> *What is man, that thou art mindful of him?*
> *And the son of man, that thou visitest him?*

Synonymous and *synthetic* parallelism not infrequently occur in the same verse, the repetition of the thought and its result being skillfully combined to give added emphasis and variety. This combination of the two forms is admirably illustrated in the opening verse of Psalm 27:

> *The Lord is my light and my salvation; whom shall I fear?*
> *The Lord is the strength of my life; of whom shall I be afraid?*

Antithetic parallelism, which is not so common as *synonymous* or *synthetic* and yet often used in the Psalms, defines itself even more clearly. Here the second half, or full line contrasts with the first by a directly opposite thought or assertion. From the many possible examples three familiar verses will suffice:

> *Weeping may endure for a night,*
> *But joy cometh in the morning.*

> *For the Lord knoweth the way of the righteous;*
> *But the way of the ungodly shall perish.*

> *A thousand shall fall at thy side,*
> *And ten thousand at thy right hand;*
> *But it shall not come nigh thee.*

Far less commonly used than these three forms, singly or in combination, and yet in no sense neglected in the Psalter is *climactic* parallelism. Sometimes this is called *stairlike*, or *step-by-step* parallelism. It repeats in the second and often in the following lines the initial words or phrases of the first, and in this way builds up its thought and its expression to a climax. It is well illustrated by Psalm 29, which, as we have seen, describes a thunder storm and which is written throughout in *climactic* parallelism:

> *Give unto the Lord, O ye mighty,*
> *Give unto the Lord glory and strength;*
> *Give unto the Lord the glory due unto his name.*

And again from the same psalm:

> *The voice of the Lord is powerful,*

The voice of the Lord is full of majesty;
The voice of the Lord breaketh the cedars;
Yea, the Lord breaketh the cedars of Lebanon.

The voice of the Lord divideth the flames of fire,
The voice of the Lord shaketh the wilderness;
The Lord shaketh the wilderness of Kadesh.

As fine an example of *climactic* parallelism is shown also in Psalm 150, which closes the Psalter with an outburst of ascending triumph.

It has been truly said that in most books of the Old Testament God speaks to men, but that in the Psalms men speak to God. This they do in all frankness, fervour, and complete honesty. Their verse form lends itself probably better than any other imaginable for their simplicity, concreteness, and vigour of human utterance. It gave them opportunity for endless, yet never wearisome repetition, for insistence, emphasis, and urgency, and, above all else, for naturalness. Always more drawn to verbs and to nouns than to many adjectives or adverbs, in both of which their language was characteristically wanting in number, they could use the unhampered, unqualified powers of these verbs and nouns to enforce a central thought, to drive home a point, and to reach a climax. They depended almost wholly upon the stress and the fall of the accents of human speech, and in so doing bequeathed to us a poetry which in its ardent, almost primitive forcefulness has had no worthy competitor, perhaps, indeed, at its best, no equal.

2

Their Thoughts and Ideas

THE HEBREW mind, as we have already seen, was not, in general, philosophical, at least in a speculative, theoretical sense, even though there have been, as we know, outstanding Jewish philosophers from Philo in the first century A.D. to men like Spinoza in the seventeenth century and like Martin Buber in our own day. This statement does not for a moment mean to imply that the Hebrew prophets and poets were not sensitive and reflective men who thought deeply about life, its questions and its problems, about God and His ways with His children. It means only that they were not given to speculation or to theory about religious and philosophical questions in that objective, abstract manner which is characteristic of the philosophic mind. And this was true simply because of their tenacious, unshakable assurance that they knew their God, because of their faith in His purposes for them as His people and for all mankind, because of their belief that He had "done great things" for them in their past and would continue to do equally great things for them in their future. Certainly there are but two books in the Old Testament which can possibly be called philosophical in the speculative, inquiring sense: the great book of Job and the lesser, yet remarkable book of Ecclesiastes. The unknown authors of both these books question the justice of God, argue and inquire into the meaning of life; one consumed by faith in spite of his suffering, bitterness, and anger, the other equally consumed by skepticism. In general, however, we do not expect nor do we get philosophizing from Hebrew poets. Instead, we get certainty in place of doubt, and, with all their candid recognition of pain, sorrow and seeming injustice, faith in place of distrust.

Of all the poetry in the Old Testament the Psalms portray most convincingly this innate character of the Hebrew mind. Their writers continually ask questions, it is true; and yet they more continually assure themselves and their readers either that they know the answers or that they do not need to know them. They lament and cry out in despair; they curse, and pray for vengeance; they wonder at the good fortunes of bad men; they hate sickness and fear death; they are overwhelmed by the mystery of life. Yet they are more overwhelmed by the greatness and the goodness of God; by the glories of His creation; by His neverfailing care and presence. The poet of Psalm 46 expresses this trust and security when he writes:

God is our refuge and strength,
A very present help in trouble.
Therefore will not we fear
Though the earth be removed,
And though the mountains be carried into the midst of the sea.

And at the conclusion of his psalm he confides the secret of the source of his faith, when, in a frequently quoted line, he puts into the words of God an appeal to men to cease their hurried, frenzied ways and to think upon higher, surer things:

Be still, and know that I am God.

Perhaps the chief contribution of the Psalms to the Old Testament as a whole lies in the extraordinary scope of their thoughts and ideas, which thoughts and ideas, in their turn, vividly illustrate the almost amazing range of Hebraic religious conceptions and also the progress and development of these as they evolved through the centuries. First and foremost among these ideas is, of course, that of God Himself. The psalmists define Him again and again, declare His attributes, His qualities, as men have seen and known them from the distant beginnings of their history throughout many periods of change and growth in thought and in belief. Indeed, of all books in the Old Testament the Psalms most completely give us an understanding of these stages of belief in God from the primitive and simple to the exalted and spiritual. Thus their poets through their wealth of material and the vividness of their imagery portray not only the religious history and the nature of a people, but also the sacredness of its Law and the teaching of its prophets. They may seem to be writing devotional poetry as, most surely, they are doing; yet in another sense they are revealing the inner life of an ancient nation over more than a thousand years.

What, then, is the nature of God as the psalmists understand Him?

In several psalms, or in portions of them (for we must always remember that many psalms are without doubt compilations rather than units of composition) God pos-

sesses anthropomorphic traits, at least in metaphor. It is entirely possible that certain of these passages which describe
the physical attributes and activity of God may have been
preserved, perhaps in a rewritten form, from ancient hymns
and psalms, now lost, which had to do with the earliest
conceptions of Him; it is far more likely, however, that such
expressions were understood by their much later authors as
metaphorical or figurative and yet as reflecting a priceless
heritage of their long faith. In such passages God has arms,
feet, mouth, ears, and nostrils. He laughs, shouts, smites,
slays, shoots arrows, whets a sword, and even drinks from a
brook. His hands prepare the dry land, and they also save
men from falling. He touches hills and they smoke. He leads
armies with thousands of chariots and goes before His
people into battle against their enemies. He is, in fact,
"mighty in battle," taking hold "of shield and buckler."
Only in the Psalms is He pictured as having wings in the
shadow of which men can hide for safety. He thunders in
the heavens as once He did in the wilderness of Mount Sinai,
sends forth hailstones, shoots forth lightnings. Such ideas,
simple and often crude as they are in themselves, retain
through the psalmists' expression of them those original
conceptions of the God of Israel as He first revealed Himself to the people whom He had chosen.

The author of Psalm 18 gives most vividly a description of
God in this primitive conception of Him:

> Then the earth shook and trembled,
> The foundations also of the hills moved and were shaken
> Because he was wroth.
> There went up a smoke out of his nostrils,
> And fire out of his mouth devoured:
> Coals were kindled by it.

He bowed the heavens also, and came down;
And darkness was under his feet.
And he rode upon a cherub and did fly:
Yea, he did fly upon the wings of the wind.
He made darkness his secret place;
His pavilion round about him were dark waters
And thick clouds of the skies.
The Lord also thundered in the heavens,
And the Highest gave his voice;
Hailstones and coals of fire.
Yea, he sent out his arrows and scattered them;
And he shot out lightnings, and discomfited them.

And yet in this same psalm there are so many other conceptions of God in His spiritual attributes that one is convinced the poet is metaphorical rather than literal in his moving and beautiful imagery. In this same poem he writes:

As for God, his way is perfect;
The word of the Lord is tried;
He is a buckler to all those that trust in him.
For who is God save the Lord?
Or who is a rock save our God?
It is God that girdeth me with strength,
And maketh my way perfect.
He maketh my feet like hinds' feet
And setteth me upon my high places.

Thy right hand hath holden me up,
And thy gentleness hath made me great.

To the psalmists God is, of course, the creator of the world, an idea common to other ancient peoples who ascribed to their god or gods the miracles of light and darkness, land and sea, moon and stars. And yet, in contrast to other minds, both ancient and modern, devout Hebrews did not believe in God merely *because they saw the wonders of His creation*. Rather they accepted and acknowledged gratefully those wonders *because they believed in Him*. In their thought God is external to His natural world, not immanent, but transcendent. To them God created the world not for itself, but for the sake of man, as the place where man could fulfill His purposes for all men or, in other words, as the setting for the drama of human life. Its wonder and beauty did not, then, exist for themselves, but as the means for a way of life which, throughout the Old Testament, is always more glorious than God's manifestation of His power as creator. All His mighty works of nature are forevermore His obedient servants, just as through His Covenant with His people He commands that they shall be obedient to His laws.

This faith in God as the creator is inevitably allied with the idea of God as the Lord of history, an idea which is, as we have seen, the most deeply rooted and unassailable belief in the Old Testament. It is the belief, in short, which underlies the claim made by the Old Testament that, through its literature, it is the witness of a people who believed with all the strength of its being that it knew the one true God. This primary assumption, that God of His own will revealed Himself to man, that He has made Himself and His purposes known through particular, concrete events and specific acts, that He is ever-present and His works ever-recurring, and that the future as well as the past is in His hands and under His control, is expressed again and again by the psalmists, sometimes in entire psalms, again in countless verses interspersed throughout the Psalter. It is, without doubt, whether expressed directly or indirectly, the most prevalent and important conception of God to be found throughout the

Psalms.

All these ideas of God, His early revelations of Himself in the beginning of the life of Israel as a nation, His creation of the cosmic universe, His acts as the Lord of history, real and tenacious though they were in the minds of the psalmists, must, however, be termed *objective* ideas when we compare them to those perceptions and beliefs about God which were most profound and secure in the hearts, affections, and loyalties of the poets who wrote our Psalter. Necessary, indeed indispensable as they were to the religious convictions of the psalmists, they were not *subjective*, that is, they did not reflect those innermost thoughts and affirmations which lay close and comforting in the imagination and in the deepest recesses of the soul.

What, then, is God in relation to a man himself? How do the psalmists know and portray Him in this most intimate sense, which Martin Buber has called the *I and Thou* relationship?

Concerning God in His relation to man there is a seeming paradox, almost a contradiction, at least in terms, which runs throughout the Old Testament in its narratives, its prophecies, and its poetry; and nowhere is this more evident than in the Psalms. Yet it did not seem paradoxical to the psalmists any more than it seemed a contradiction to the patriarchs, the prophets, and the kings. On the one hand, God is *remote, mysterious, afar off, hidden, absent, distant,* the *King of kings,* the *Lord of lords,* the *High and Holy One.* He is *majestic* and *awesome, mighty* and *terrible.* He "sitteth between the cherubims," writes the poet of Psalm 99; He "is mightier than the noise of many waters," exclaims the writer of Psalm 93. On the other hand, God is *near, known, familiar, revealed, constantly present,* and even *intimate.* He is alike the *friend* and the *strength* of men. He not only yearns over His children, but He suffers with them in their sorrows. High though He is, "yet He hath respect unto the lowly" and "healeth the broken in heart."

To all the psalmists this *remoteness* and this *nearness* are inseparable in the true nature of God; and yet it is in His nearness, in Him as personal and approachable, that they constantly place their invulnerable faith. The poet of Psalm 73 cries:

> *Whom have I in heaven but thee?*
> *And there is none upon earth that I desire beside thee.*
> *My flesh and my heart faileth;*
> *But God is the strength of my heart*
> *And my portion for ever.*

And he is echoed by the writer of Psalm 63:

> *Because thy lovingkindness is better than life,*
> *My lips shall praise thee.*
> *Thus will I bless thee while I live;*
> *I will lift up my hands in thy name.*
> *My soul shall be satisfied with marrow and fatness,*
> *And my mouth shall praise thee with joyful lips*
> *When I remember thee upon my bed*
> *And meditate on thee in the night watches.*
> *Because thou hast been my help,*
> *Therefore in the shadow of thy wings will I rejoice.*

The most outstanding characteristic of God in the words and thoughts of the psalmists is his *lovingkindness*. This noun is used again and again. The Hebrew term for it is *chesedh*, and it is a word very difficult to translate accurately into English. Sometimes it is rendered as *mercy*, although *lovingkindness* has a more personal connotation. It surely contains the suggestion of *compassion* and even of *companionship*. Perhaps this last-named quality, *companionship*, is the most inherent element in *lovingkindness* since the Hebrew word *chesedh* is inseparable from the sense of a *covenant*, an *agreement*, an *understanding* between God and man. This idea of active participation in the daily affairs of men, this common life shared by God and His people, had been emphasized by the great Hebrew prophets, Amos, Hosea, Micah, Isaiah, and Jeremiah, two and three centuries before most of the psalms were written. Perhaps nothing in the Old Testament is more appealing than are these concrete and personal images of God in relation with His children. He is pictured as a member of their families, as a father, a husband, or a brother. He is, of course, a shepherd, as they themselves were shepherds and as their forefathers had been. He is a farmer sifting out the wheat; a builder holding a plumbline; a potter working in clay at his wheel. He is a scribe, writing His Law in the hearts of men, and a physician healing the sick. He is even a common water-seller in the market-place.

Thus no occupation known by men and women in their daily lives is unknown to Him; nor are any human emotions unfamiliar or unfelt. He can be indignant and angry as well as forbearing and compassionate, sorrowful as well as glad, scornful as well as approving, impatient as well as patient. The psalmists, therefore, in their portrayal of Him as a loving and always a personal God were but echoing and completing in their own imagery a conception which is the basic conviction of the prophets and, indeed, of the entire Old Testament from the stories of the Creation and the Covenant at Sinai to the latest of its prophets and poets and to the last of its books.

But if God participates in the life of man, even in all its homely details and problems, so man in the thought of the psalmists must in his turn participate in the life of God. With his whole being he must strive to obey God's commandments, to be faithful to His holy laws. This Law of God is in the Psalms, interpreted in two ways: (1) as the Law given originally from Mount Sinai to Moses and centuries later, around 400 B.C., at about the time when at least some of the psalms were written, had been codified and published with all its traditions and later accretions and with all its exact demands as to sacrifices and conduct; and (2) as the law in the sense of man's moral, ethical, and religious attitude and behaviour toward his fellowmen rather than in the sense of scrupulous obedience to external commands.

The first interpretation of the Law is expressed in Psalm 1, which is an introduction, largely in prose, to the Psalms as a book:

Blessed is the man that walketh not in the counsel of the ungodly, nor standeth in the way of sinners, nor sitteth in the seat of the scornful. But his delight is in the Law of the Lord; and in his Law doth he meditate day and night.

This Law, divinely bestowed upon Israel, is again extolled in Psalm 19; yet one notes at once that it is truly a "delight" and not a burden:

The law of the Lord is perfect, converting the soul,
The testimony of the Lord is sure, making wise the simple.
The statutes of the Lord are right, rejoicing the heart;
The commandment of the Lord is pure, enlightening the eyes.
The fear of the Lord is clean, enduring for ever;
The judgments of the Lord are true and righteous altogether.

And much of Psalm 119 in its twenty-two sections, named
for the letters of the Hebrew alphabet, has to do with faithful obedience to the demands of this written and established
Law.

Nevertheless, although the psalmists quite clearly think
that all men under God's Law should pay heed to its outward
observances, it is the second understanding of His commands which is more binding upon them. In Psalm 51,
where certain sacrifices and other outward observances are
clearly suggested, the psalmist toward the close of his poem
declares:

For thou desirest not sacrifice; else would I give it;
Thou delightest not in burnt offering.
The sacrifices of God are a broken spirit;
A broken and a contrite heart, O God, thou wilt not despise.

And the poet of Psalm 40 repeats the same thought when he
says that God does not desire sacrifice and offering so much
as He desires righteousness and truth.

Only second to God's *lovingkindness*, His tenderness and
care for the individual, is in the mind of the psalmist His
righteousness and *justice*. This great theme of the prophets
is echoed again and again throughout the Psalms. The author
of Psalm 97 pictures God in all His glory, yet with His
righteousness even more emphasized:

Clouds and darkness are round about him;
Righteousness and judgment are the habitation of his throne.

Psalm 85 sees in Him all truth and justice, mercy, righteousness and peace:

Mercy and truth are met together;
Righteousness and peace have kissed each other.
Truth shall spring out of the earth;
And righteousness shall look down from heaven.

In Psalms 7, 9, and 96, to name but a few, His righteous judgments are extolled. To these poets He is incapable of injustice, for "he shall minister judgment to the people in uprightness."

Nor must we for a moment imagine that this *righteousness*, this *justice* of God, was considered in any abstract way by the psalmists. Again like the prophets before them they thought of righteousness not as merely an idea, or as an ideal which might exist outside or above the world of affairs and of action, but, instead, as a concrete, constantly operative act. Throughout the Psalms God has performed, is performing, and will continue to perform righteous and just acts; and He requires, indeed *demands*, that those who are bound by faith and covenant to Him must themselves perform righteous acts in their daily lives and toward their fellowmen. Righteousness is, then, the standard of thought and of behaviour which God maintains in the world, the standard by which He judges men.

And now what of men themselves? How did the psalmists look upon the world of human affairs? What thoughts and ideas filled their minds as they looked upon themselves in relation to God and upon the seeming injustice in the world? What did they think of sin, of the good man and of the wicked, of the problem of pain and sorrow, of life and of death? All these conceptions and questions occur countless times in the Psalms just as they have been from the beginning in the minds of all thoughtful men.

First of all, what to them is sin? It is, of course, transgres-

sion against God in the performing of wrong or unjust acts
or even in the thought of such performance. Many of the
psalmists recognize such transgression and beg God's forgiveness and redemption:

Have mercy upon me, O God, according to thy lovingkindness,
According unto the multitude of thy tender mercies, blot out
  my transgressions.
Wash me thoroughly from my iniquity,
And cleanse me from my sin;
For I acknowledge my transgressions,
And my sin is ever before me.

And again:

> *For I will declare mine iniquity;*
> *I will be sorry for my sin.*

They recognize also, as did the author of Job, both that
all men are by nature erring and sinful and that even when
sin is not clearly discerned, it may well lurk within the
heart. The psalmist of Psalm 130 makes this first thought
clear when he questions:

> *If thou, Lord, shouldst mark iniquities,*
> *O Lord, who shall stand?*

In the same way does the writer of Psalm 51 when he cries
in despair that he, like all men, "was shapen in iniquity."
Secret sins weigh upon their minds in several passages in
which they beg to be freed from faults not clearly realized
by themselves and yet known to God. Most familiar among
these are the words of Psalm 19:

> *Who can understand his errors?*
> *Cleanse thou me from secret faults.*

And those as well of Psalm 139:

> *Search me, O God, and know my heart;*
> *Try me, and know my thoughts;*
> *And see if there be any wicked way in me,*
> *And lead me in the way everlasting.*

The most painful of sins, however, to the psalmists, and surely the worst in its enormity, is, as it was to the prophets before them, rebellion against God, wilful separation from Him, indifference, apathy, carelessness. "The rebellious dwell in a dry land"; they "will not seek after God"; they "are like the chaff which the wind driveth away." Such separation from God, such denial of His constant care and presence, such deafness and blindness to His commands and purposes for men, is the most unforgivable of sins; and the psalmists pray constantly to be freed from that desolation just as they constantly thank God for His nearness:

> *The wicked . . . will not seek after God;*
> *God is not in all his thoughts.*
> *Arise, O Lord, O God, lift up thine hand,*
> *Forget not the humble.*

> *Forsake me not, O Lord.*
> *O My God, be not far from me.*
> *Make haste to help me,*
> *O Lord of my salvation.*

And they cry in gratitude and trust:

> *The sun shall not smite thee by day*
> *Nor the moon by night.*

The Lord shall preserve thee from all evil,
He shall preserve thy soul.

I will lay me down in peace and sleep,
For thou, Lord, only makest me to dwell in safety.

Many, if not most of the psalmists are deeply concerned with the apparent good fortune of the wicked, who, according to one poet, flourishes "like a green bay tree." In spite of the firm teaching of the Law, which declares that the good are rewarded by God, whereas punishment is meted out by Him to the wicked, their daily experience has proved to them that the rebellious man often prospers in the things of this life, that, indeed, "the wicked spring as the grass." From the almost numberless verses in the many psalms given to this mystery, one realizes that it was a question always bewildering, yet always hidden from human understanding. It is doubtless true that most of the psalmists accepted the traditional teaching with all its difficulties. Did not Psalm 1 affirm that "the way of the ungodly shall perish," and what was the mind of mere man against the revealed Law of God?

A sense of resignation almost fatalistic is expressed by the author of Psalm 39, who is obviously profoundly distressed although he clearly has no solution:

I said, I will take heed to my ways
That I sin not with my tongue.
I will keep my mouth with a bridle
While the wicked is before me.
I was dumb with silence,
I held my peace, even from good,
And my sorrow was stirred.

Lord, make me to know mine end,

And the measure of my days, what it is,
That I may know how frail I am.
Behold, thou hast made my days as a handbreadth,
And mine age is as nothing before thee.
Verily, every man at his last state is altogether vanity.

In a few psalms, however, there *are* attempts at a solution. The writer of Psalm 37, the man responsible for the image of the green bay tree, in his poem of forty verses all of which deal with the problem, says again and again that the wealth and prosperity of the wicked are merely transitory and unreal and that the sword with which they have "cut down the poor and the needy" must finally "enter into their own hearts." Like the writer of Psalm 112 he concludes that, however things may seem to the outward eye, however the good man may be outraged by this seeming injustice, in the end evil-doers must be cut off and that the righteous must not only be blessed but continue "in everlasting remembrance." And in all the psalmists who are troubled by this apparent refutation not only of the Holy Law, but of God's Covenant with His people, there is expressed explicitly or implicitly the knowledge that God alone is the reward of the righteous man, that nearness to Him is life whereas separation from Him is death. In other words, they affirm that the goodness of man's life with God and the evil of life without Him should blot out all thought of earthly and outward compensation. The love of God for the sake of God is in itself enough.

It is this final conclusion which is expressed in the closing verses of Psalm 73:

Whom have I in heaven but thee?
And there is none upon earth that I desire beside thee.

My flesh and my heart faileth;
But God is the strength of my heart,
And my portion for ever.
For, lo, they that are far from thee shall perish . . .
But it is good for me to draw near to God.

In the book of Job, which in probable date was relatively contemporaneous with at least some of the psalms, there is seemingly expressed the hope of a future life, even the faith that there is such a reward for unfailing trust in God. This may be only a fancy, or at most a momentary conviction in the mind of Job, to whom God's love and goodness are so sure and certain that death as an utter finality to life, death which removes a man forever from that love, seems incredible. As all scholars of the book recognize, the text of Job is so difficult of translation and in places so linguistically confused that one cannot be entirely sure whether Job is asserting that God will vindicate him on earth *before* his death or whether he is declaring his belief that *after* his death he will see God for himself. In the early chapters of this great book, especially in the third chapter, Job looks forward only to the silence and the peace of death, when he shall lie still and be at rest. Later, however, he affirms his knowledge of the immortality of his "Redeemer" and his assurance that even without his tortured, earthly body he "shall see God." Whether this assurance is that of a single individual, in agony and yet in triumphant faith, who is convinced that the love and care of God must endure beyond this earth; whether Job's words must be interpreted as his conviction that his faith must be fully recognized by God *before* his death; or whether from the teaching of the religious faith of his people and of his day he accepted no actual resurrection of the body or of the soul—all these questions seem impossible of any definite or conclusive answer.

Surely at the time of the writing of Job and of the Psalms any doctrine of the resurrection of the body or of the soul was not included or allowed in the teaching of Israel. Such doctrine among certain circles came many years later, long after Job was written and probably long after the dates of most, if not all of the psalms. What, then, can we honestly discover in the Psalms, as a book, which assumes any belief in an after life?

Practically all the psalmists see death as the end of life and the dead as those whom God "remembereth no more." Psalm 98 asks almost bitterly:

> *Shall thy lovingkindness be declared in the grave?*
> *Or thy faithfulness in destruction?*
> *Shall thy wonders be known in the dark?*
> *And thy righteousness in the land of forgetfulness?*

And Psalm 115 adds:

> *The dead praise not the Lord,*
> *Neither any that go down into silence.*

Unquestionably the psalmists in general did not believe in active immortality, in any resurrection of the body or of the soul. The only immortality assured to a good man was the value of his righteous acts and the continuance of his memory in the minds of those who had known him. In accordance with the religious teaching in which they had been reared they accepted the belief expressed or implied throughout the Old Testament: At death the soul descended to Hell, *Sheol* in their Hebraic term, a dim region very like the Greek Hades in which there was no consciousness of a previous existence and where God remembered no one. No psalmist has expressed this acceptance more clearly or more beautifully than the great poet of Psalm 90:

> *The days of our years are threescore years and ten,*
> *And if by reason of strength they be fourscore years,*
> *Yet is their strength labour and sorrow,*
> *For it is soon cut off, and we fly away.*

In view of this belief, therefore, the thought and the hope which animate the psalmists are the thought and the hope of a long life. The promise of God made by the writer of Psalm 91,

> *With long life will I satisfy him,*
> *And shew him my salvation,*

describes the state most desired by all men. And this hope is repeated in several other psalms. In Psalm 92:

> *They shall still bring forth fruit in old age,*
> *They shall be fat and flourishing.*

In Psalm 41:

> *The Lord will preserve him and keep him alive,*
> *And he shall be blessed upon the earth.*

Sickness throughout the Psalms is always deplored, and death is hated and feared, its "darkness" and its "shadow." "The dead praise not the Lord," writes the author of Psalm 115; the discouraged and ill man in Psalm 31 describes himself as "forgotten out of mind," as one who is dead.

Certain scholars, however, and excellent ones, have discovered in a few psalms, notably Psalms 16, 49, and 73, at
least hopes of immortality. In Psalm 16:

> *For thou wilt not leave my soul in Hell. . . .*
> *Thou wilt show me the path of life;*
> *In thy presence is fullness of joy;*
> *At thy right hand there are pleasures for evermore.*

In Psalm 49:

But God will redeem my soul from the powers of the grave;
For he shall receive me.

And in Psalm 73:

> *Nevertheless I am continually with thee,*
> *Thou hast holden me by my right hand.*
> *Thou shall guide me with thy counsel,*
> *And afterward receive me to glory.*

Perhaps the most honest position which the reader of the
Psalms can take concerning these hopes or glimpses of a
future life for man is neither to accept them completely nor
wholly to deny them. The men who cherished them may,
like Job, have been themselves consumed by a longer vision,
a surer hope; or they may have been individuals capable of
aspiration and faith not generally possessed in their day.
There are always such personalities in every age.

As a collection of devotional poetry, however, the Psalms
have little, or perhaps even nothing, to do with the unknown
future of the human soul. With all their wealth of thoughts
and ideas, many of which vividly illustrate the range and
the development of the religion of ancient Israel, their chief

concern is with God Himself in His relation to mankind upon this earth. Their poets write of God as remote and terrible, God as close at hand and companionable, God as King, God as Father, and, above all else, God as necessary and indispensable to one's life simply because He is God.

We may well conclude this chapter on the thoughts and ideas in the Psalms by a brief consideration or study of one of the finest in the entire collection, Psalm 19, a psalm, of course, familiar to many if not to most readers. This beautiful psalm, which I am including here for convenient study, has been the subject of much controversy on the part of scholars, many of whom contend that it is clearly no unit of composition, but, instead, a compilation, that its three distinct parts must have been written by different poets or at least, if by one poet, as units and later assembled as one psalm.

Psalm 19

1–6

The heavens declare the glory of God;
And the firmament sheweth his handiwork.
Day unto day uttereth speech,
And night unto night sheweth knowledge.
There is no speech nor language
Where their voice is not heard.
Their line is gone out through all the earth,
And their words to the end of the world.
In them hath he set a tabernacle for the sun,
Which is as a bridegroom coming out of his chamber,

And rejoiceth as a strong man to run a race.
His going forth is from the end of the heaven,
And his circuit unto the ends of it,
And there is nothing hid from the heat thereof.

7–11

The law of the Lord is perfect, converting the soul:
The testimony of the Lord is sure, making wise the simple.
The statutes of the Lord are right, rejoicing the heart:
The commandment of the Lord is pure, enlightening the eyes.
The fear of the Lord is clean, enduring for ever:
The judgments of the Lord are true and righteous altogether.
More to be desired are they than gold, yea, than much fine gold:
Sweeter also than honey and the honeycomb.
Moreover by them is thy servant warned:
And in keeping of them there is great reward.

12–14

Who can understand his errors?
Cleanse thou me from secret faults.
Keep back thy servant also from presumptuous sins;
Let them not have dominion over me:
Then shall I be upright,
And I shall be innocent from the great transgression.
Let the words of my mouth, and the meditation of my heart,
Be acceptable in thy sight, O Lord,
My strength, and my redeemer.

As one reads the psalm, there seem to be good reasons for the conclusion of the scholars. The three obvious divisions do seem each unique in itself: the first on the glory of God's creation, His heavens, their speech, which echoes throughout His earth by day and by night, His sun, from the heat and light of which nothing is hid; the second, a poem in honour of His sacred Law; the third, a personal, fervent

prayer of supplication that a man's words and thoughts may
be acceptable in His sight. Even the verse form, the careful
stanzaic structure of each distinct part, the differing length
and stress of the lines, would seem to bear out the opinion
that we have here three short psalms instead of one, and
perhaps by three quite different psalmists.

Still, when we look more carefully, when we study the
psalm in its entirety and especially in relation to those
thoughts and ideas which were closest to the Hebrew mind,
does it necessarily suggest three units of composition? May
it not be, instead, a single psalm written precisely as it is in
order to convey perhaps a subtle, yet strong, even powerful
meaning? In other words, does it not give a true portrait of
the religious conceptions and values of ancient Israel in
terms of God and man in their ever-present, indissoluble
partnership?

In its first part, God as Creator of a wondrous universe is
extolled; in its second part, the poet is concerned with the
perfection of his Lord as it is revealed in His Law, divinely
given to man and never to be forgotten; and in its third
part, he becomes conscious of himself and his own relation
to that wonder and to that perfection. He is but a man who
does not always understand his mistakes, who is not always
aware of his "secret faults"; and he pleads as do other psalmists that his words and his thoughts may be acceptable to
God, his Maker and his friend, and that he may never forget
the glory of the Lord whether in His Creation, His Law, or
in His constant care for men.

It seems to me that no other psalm in our book as a whole
presents so clear a picture of the mind of all the psalmists,
in terms of their thinking, their wonder, their sense of obligation, their invulnerable faith. Perhaps its author, glowing

with his various conceptions of God, wrote it in three parts, at different times—who can know?—and then realized himself that all its parts really belonged *together*, that each portrayed his God and his Lord, and, above all else, that the sight of God's wonders and the praise of His Law were not in themselves enough without a dedication of the human soul, of himself in all humility and longing.

Thus this poet of Psalm 19 has solved the seeming paradox of the nature of God. God is at once remote and close, intangible yet tangible. Man knows Him as his "strength and redeeemer" not alone by observing His wonders or by obeying His statutes, right as they are, but by searching his own heart in order to see whether he himself is acceptable in his own life or whether sins of presumption and indifference can blind his vision of his God.

3

Their Literary Devices

IN THE title of this final chapter of my book about the Psalms I have purposely used the term *literary devices* instead of *literary traits*. *Traits* is too large and inclusive a word for my desires and aims, which are to show the ways and means employed by the best of the psalmists to endow their songs and poems with enduring life, even with a liveliness and an excitement still real and vibrant after more than two thousand years. I am, of course, fully aware of the fact that the word *devices* suggests *contrivance*, perhaps even *tricks* of style or of diction, and that it suggests also the admission on the part of the psalmists that they are purposely employing words, images, figures, and sentence structure in such a way as to appeal to their listeners or to their readers; in other words, that their art is artificial and carefully designed for effect.

Well, why not? All honest writers know that art is artificial rather than "inspirational," that effects are carefully planned and designed, that words are sifted, scrutinized and meticulously chosen, that sentences are studied and weighed before they are set down on paper. When the Latin poet Horace wrote just before the beginning of the Christian era, *Ars est celare artem,* or "Art is to conceal art," he was but telling the truth about all who deal in words. He meant, of course, that the simplest and seemingly the most natural and spontaneous of literary expression is, nevertheless, most carefully prepared, that although the reader is impressed, as the writer hoped he would be, and perhaps even disarmed by apparent artlessness, the art, or the craft, is there, concealed though it often is.

Horace probably knew nothing whatever about the Hebrew psalmists; yet he characterizes them especially aptly. For drama was inherent in the Hebraic nature, although, perhaps oddly, it is the one type of literature lacking in the Old Testament, at least in outward form. All Old Testament narratives teem with dramatic elements, however, as does all its poetry. It would be absurd to think that the psalmists were not aware of the ways and means provided them both by their language and their verse form and by the richness and vitality of themselves to impress their readers, to secure interest and attention, to make truth more true. To them, as to the prophets, and the story-tellers before them, nothing was ever ordinary, worn, tarnished, taken for granted. Instead, everything was alive with the Reality of God; and it was this reality which they longed to convey.

The very candour with which they write, the fact that they are, in every conceivable mood, pouring out their hearts to God, the fact, too, that the form of their verse resembles more than any other the accents of human speech —all these point unmistakably to their desire and their labour to frame their words and thoughts in such a way that other hearts and minds may share their emotions. They were, of course, "inspired" as all artists are inspired by Powers mysteriously granted to them; and yet they knew, as all artists have always known, those ways and means, those methods and devices, which could best insure the effects which they longed to secure.

We have already seen how the spendthrift author of Psalm 27 exhausted the possibilities of his language and its construction in order to gain the strength and the variety which he so intensely wanted for his great poem. No one would question the fact of his inspired faith; and yet all must acknowledge his acute awareness of the means by which that faith might be best brought home to both faithful and faithless alike.

Of all those literary devices recognized and used again and again by the psalmists—repetition, imagery, swift changes in sentence structure, comparison and contrast, variety in stress and in length of line—two stand out because of their frequency and because in themselves they illustrate so clearly the imagination of the poets who used them to such fine effect. The first is the use of the simile or the metaphor; the second, the employment of the question. These two I shall try to illustrate more fully.

The similes and metaphors of the psalmists, without which their work would lose much of its richness and appeal, are drawn, of course, from the life they knew, from their countryside, the familiar sights and sounds among which they had been reared. By their use of these they hoped to bring home hidden meanings, to clarify, heighten, and intensify their thoughts, to clothe the common with such significance that it became uncommon, took on added stature, touched an answering chord in those who heard their words.

The dwellers in ancient Israel, we must always remember,

were a hill people. They knew little about the sea, even the
Mediterranean, which lay beyond their western coastal plain.
The ocean, as we understand the term, was completely unknown to them. Unlike the Greeks or their neighbours, the
Phoenicians, they were in no sense sailors or seafarers. In
the Psalms there are hardly more than a dozen references to
the sea, and these are consistently expressions of awe and
wonder, often containing more than a suggestion of fear:

> *So is this great and wide sea*
> *Wherein are things creeping innumerable,*
> *Both small and great beasts.*

> *They that go down to the sea in ships,*
> *That do business in great waters;*
> *These see the works of the Lord,*
> *And his wonders in the deep.*
> *For he commandeth and raiseth the stormy wind,*
> *Which lifteth up the waves thereof.*
> *They mount to the heaven,*
> *They go down again to the depths;*
> *They reel to and fro,*
> *And stagger like a drunken man,*
> *And are at their wits' end.*

The Lord, to be sure, "rulest the raging of the sea," and He
is "mightier than the mighty waves"; yet there is not one
among the psalmists who draws near to Him because of this
power, always both foreign and fearful to them. The sea,
like those upon it, was "afar off" in their consciousness.
Instead, they liken God to the mountains which they knew
and loved, to the everlasting hills, their sure and familiar
home, toward which they lift their eyes and from whence
comes their help. The Psalms would be poorer, indeed, with-

out these many comparisons to mountains and hills, which, in bright, concrete, personified imagery, skip like rams and lambs, leap, and praise God just as the valleys between and among them shout for joy and sing. God is "the strength of the hills," which are "joyful" because of His presence; and His mountains "bring peace to the people."

> *Thy righteousness is like the great mountains,*

writes the psalmist of Psalm 36; and the author of Psalm 125 continues the simile in one of the most lovely comparisons of the entire Psalter:

> *As the mountains are round about Jerusalem,*
> *So the Lord is round about his people*
> *From henceforth even for ever.*

In a dry, hot, barren land great rocks meant a hiding-place from the burning sun, a chance for shade and shadow, a resting-place for the wayfarer. God sets a man's stumbling feet upon a rock; He is constantly declared to be the "rock of salvation." The psalmist of Psalm 62 is not content with likening Him once to a rock, but must compare Him three times to this rude strength and help which he knows so well:

> *He only is my rock and my salvation;*
> *He is my defence; I shall not be moved.*

And the writer of Psalm 18 is quite as generous in his similar comparisons, which are echoed in Psalms 28, 31, 42, and 61, to name but a few.

Trees were rare in the land of Israel. Like rocks they, too, meant shade and rest from the torrid heat. Did the author of

Psalm 1, who compares the good man to "a tree planted by the rivers of water" know Jeremiah's identical words written or spoken perhaps two or three centuries earlier? Not only does God Himself plant the cedars of Lebanon, not only are all His trees "full of sap," that is, alive and flourishing; but His trees "rejoice" before Him, knowing that they also are created by Him for the refreshment of men.

God knows the birds, too, and cares for them:

> *For every beast of the forest is mine,*
> *And the cattle upon a thousand hills.*
> *I know all the fowls of the air;*
> *And the wild beasts of the fields are mine.*

The psalmist longs to "flee as a bird"; he wishes he had "wings like a dove"; he is ecstatic when he sees the sparrows and swallows building their untidy nests even in the stones of God's altars; through God's mercy he has escaped danger "as a bird out of the snare of the fowlers."

Bees and their honey are not forgotten by the psalmists. Doubtless they remembered the many references to honey in the old stories of their people: the manna in the wilderness which tasted like honey; Jonathan's taste of the wild honey which "enlightened" his eyes; the honey which was used for cakes; the honey which Jacob sent to Joseph in Egypt; the land promised to their forefathers which should be rich in olive oil and honey. One of them in Psalm 19 compares God's judgments to the sweetness of "honey and the honeycomb"; and another in Psalm 119 likens His words to the same familiar gift.

Because water was so scarce in their land, because the farmers were dependent only on the former rains of the autumn and the latter rains of the spring, the psalmist often thanks God for rain which, he says, refreshes the weary and allows them to "go from strength to strength." The writer of Psalm 72 compares Him to welcome showers:

> *He shall come down like rain upon the mown grass,*
> *As showers that water the earth.*

And the author of Psalm 42 describes himself as a thirsty hart desperate for a drink:

> *As the hart panteth after the water brooks,*
> *So panteth my soul after thee, O God.*

Sheep and their shepherds are common subjects for similes and metaphors. Psalms 79, 95, and 100 use almost identical words in picturing God's people as "the sheep of his pasture" or of "his hand"; and the author of the final stanza of Psalm 119 says that he has "gone astray like a lost sheep." Psalm 23, as we all know, carries the familiar metaphor throughout its six beautiful verses.

Nor do all the similes in the Psalms come from the more serene and beneficent aspects of country life. Some quite naturally express the dangers and the fears on every side. Recalling without doubt the hot winds that swept their land, certain psalmists see all people as driven before the winds or as grass which is tossed away. Their enemies to them lurk in secret places "like lions" which raven and roar; and they pray that they themselves may be saved "from the lion's mouth."

Other figures have to do with the simple, homely objects of their households, garments, lamps, lights, and candles. All people must "wax old like a garment"; and yet God covers Himself "with light as with a garment." Candles, lamps, and lights are frequently used. These all without doubt meant to the psalmists the same object, a small earthern lamp in which a wick floating in oil gave a flickering light. God's word is "as a lamp" to the writer of Psalm 119; and the author of Psalm 18 says that God will light his candle in the darkness. Even the lowly moth is not forgotten, but is used to describe the wasting away of the presumptuous man, whom God is correcting for his vanity.

These figures in the Psalms not only add immeasurably to their charm as poetry, but they also serve to tell us something at least about the life of their day, its pursuits and its values. As we have seen from reading our account of the history of Israel, the centuries in which many psalms were written is a closed book so far as actual historical knowledge is concerned. Nor does the Old Testament itself tell us anything clearly about life as it was lived by men and women in general after the Return from Exile, when Israel, once a proud kingdom and even a small empire under David and Solomon, was now but a province in subjection, first to Persia and afterward to the overlords of Alexander of Macedon, who in 332 B.C. became its conqueror. We know only that it was a small settlement, clearly a negligible item in the great Persian and Hellenistic empires. Most of its distinctly Jewish people lived, if they were able to do so, in or within a radius of a few miles of Jerusalem in the small province of Judea. The Temple, rebuilt, as we have seen, around 516 B.C. on the ruins of Solomon's Temple, was its religious center.

The Psalms would at least suggest that the Judean community was one of farmers, small tradesmen, and artisans, merchants, potters, weavers, smiths and other workers in metal. Fields, pastures, and vineyards are mentioned more

often than are other places of work. The psalmist of Psalm
144 prays that garners may be full, that sheep may bring
forth abundantly, and that oxen may be strong in their
labour. If God will but bring these things to pass, His
people will once more be happy. And the writer of Psalm
107 writes of fields, vineyards, and flourishing cattle as
blessings of God.

We know, however, or perhaps gather, from the last
chapters of the book of Isaiah, written probably between
400 and 300 B.C. and from certain of the so-called minor
prophets, that life was not too joyous or even easy, that
droughts were common, that trade languished, that the
problem of intermarriage with aliens was a source of deep
anxiety, and that, all in all, the life of the returned exiles was
a struggling and troubled one. Foreign influences were
strong, and clearly apostasy from the old faith wrought
havoc among the weaker, more easily swayed dwellers in
Judea as well as in neighbouring areas. Were the Psalms
written, as certain scholars maintain, by a group of deeply
religious Israelites, bent above everything else on keeping
the Law alive and active in the midst of hostile influences
both from conquerors and from neighbours? This we cannot truly know. But it is easy to assume or to imagine that
the "enemies" who figure so largely in their laments, both
national and personal, and in other psalms as well were the
people among them or on their borders who were a mixed
race, and who either did not share their religious faith or
were careless and apathetic in the observances commanded
by the Law.

Throughout the Psalms one is frequently made aware of
the intense honour and value always accorded to the family
and to the home as a unit of solidarity, security, and

strength. God again and again is likened to a father. He is "a father of the fatherless"; "a judge of the widows"; He "setteth the solitary in families."

> *Like as a father pitieth his children,*
> *So the Lord pitieth them that fear him.*

God makes the barren woman "to keep house" and to be "a joyful mother of children." The happy man is he who eats the labour of his hands, whose wife is "like a fruitful vine" by the sides of his house, and whose children are "like olive plants" around his table. Men long for sons who may be "as plants grown up in their youth" and for daughters "as corner stones, polished after the similitude of a palace."

No one could honestly claim that the Psalms are rich in social significance, that they in any sense clearly depict the life of their day. Yet through their similes and metaphors one *can* glean more than a little about the values which those who wrote, read, or sang them held most dear; about the things which they loved; and about the daily affairs which most deeply concerned them. Without such comparisons to their countryside, to their labour, to the people who surrounded them, and to their homes the psalmists as poets of their time would be far less vivid than they are.

And now what about the second literary device which is employed again and again, not only to add drama and excitement to the Psalms, but also to secure the fullest attention of their readers,—the use of the question?

Questions occur throughout the Old Testament, and not only in its poetry. They are used repeatedly in its narratives to heighten interest there also; *"Where is the lamb for a burnt offering?"* asks the innocent boy Isaac of his father as they approach the mountain of sacrifice. *"The child is not;*

and I—whither shall I go?" cries the frightened Reuben,
when he discovers that Joseph is no longer in the pit. Leah
screams at Rachel: *"Is it a small matter that thou hast taken
my husband? And wouldest thou take away my son's man-
drakes also?"* *"Why are his chariots so long in coming?"*
begs the distraught mother of Sisera as she gazes from her
window. *"Can I bring him back again?"* asks the remorseful
David when he learns that his child is dead. *"What sawest
thou?"* asks the defeated and hopeless King Saul of the wise
woman of Endor in her cave.

Such questions and hundreds like them not only endow
the Old Testament characters with reality and humanity,
but they also suggest the mystery which surrounds all human life and toward which the many writers of the Old
Testament were always sensitive. God impresses upon Job
this mystery by the almost ruthless succession of mighty
questions which He asks of Job in the final chapters of that
great book. The unknown poet of Job, indeed, realizing that
life itself is a quest or a search, veiled in mystery and never
truly discovered or answered, makes his whole superb poem
a question.

Surely the psalmists knew precisely what they were
doing, what sense of compassion and companionship they
were inducing in other men, when they asked their many
questions, not only of God, but of themselves.

> *Why art thou cast down, O my soul?*
> *And why art thou disquieted within me?*

twice asks the poet of Psalm 42–43, thus expressing the
frequent despair of all who live and suffer. And, like many
other questioners among the psalmists, he answers himself
with that tenacious trust which was always returning to

them like the rains of autumn and of spring:

> *Hope thou in God: for I shall yet praise him,*
> *Who is the health of my countenance, and my God.*

> *How shall we sing the Lord's song in a strange land?*

cries the poet of Psalm 137, an ancient question, but one which through many centuries has voiced the tragedy and the sadness of an entire race, from its beginnings even until now.

The writer of Psalm 10 allows bitterness and desperation to creep into his questions when he asks:

> *Why standest thou afar off, O Lord?*
> *Why hidest thou thyself in times of trouble?*

as does the poet of Psalm 22 in his familiar, terrible cry:

> *My God, my God, why hast thou forsaken me?*
> *Why art thou so far from helping me?*

The author of Psalm 15, on the contrary, is simple, almost naïve in his plaintive, childlike words:

> *Lord, who shall abide in thy tabernacle?*
> *Who shall dwell in thy holy hill?*

And the sadly puzzled writer of Psalm 44 brings his heart into the accents of his voice when he asks and pleads:

> *Why sleepest thou, O Lord?*
> *Arise, cast us not off for ever.*

These differing moods of the psalmists, these echoes of their distress, or their fear, or their bewilderment, appeal to

us all as their numberless exclamations, clearly their favourite literary device, can never do. For through their frank
and spontaneous questions they have brought many generations of readers to a deeper understanding of both suffering
and safety, and of those eternal doubts and fears, hopes and
desires, which are the common lot of all who wonder over
the mysterious ways of God with men.

Perhaps among them the psalmist of Psalm 139 has sur-
passed all other questioners, partly in the beauty of his
language, largely in his ingenuous wonder which mark both
his questions and his surprised assurance:

> *Whither shall I go from thy spirit?*
> *Or whither shall I flee from thy presence?*
> *If I ascend up into heaven, thou art there.*
> *If I make my bed in hell, behold, thou art there.*
> *If I take the wings of the morning,*
> *And dwell in the uttermost parts of the sea,*
> *Even there shall thy hand lead me,*
> *And thy right hand shall hold me.*

PART THREE

Supplement

1

Types of Psalms

Author's note: The psalms quoted in the following pages are arranged according to the form given in the Authorized or King James Version. This is done because most readers are more familiar with it through the reading of their own Bibles. In the chapters of the book itself the verses are broken into their poetic lines.

HYMNS

PSALM 8

O LORD our Lord, how excellent *is* thy name in all the earth! who hast set thy glory above the heavens.

2 Out of the mouth of babes and sucklings hast thou ordained strength because of thine enemies, that thou mightest still the enemy and the avenger.

3 When I consider thy heavens, the work of thy fingers, the moon and the stars, which thou hast ordained;

4 What is man, that thou art mindful of him? and the son of man, that thou visitest him?

5 For thou hast made him a little lower than the angels, and hast crowned him with glory and honour.

6 Thou madest him to have dominion over the works of thy hands; thou hast put all *things* under his feet:

7 All sheep and oxen, yea, and the beasts of the field;

8 The fowl of the air, and the fish of the sea, *and whatsoever* passeth through the paths of the seas.

9 O Lord our Lord, how excellent *is* thy name in all the earth!

PSALM 95

O COME, let us sing unto the Lord: let us make a joyful noise to the rock of our salvation.

2 Let us come before his presence with thanksgiving, and make a joyful noise unto him with psalms.

3 For the Lord *is* a great God, and a great King above all gods.

4 In his hand *are* the deep places of the earth: the strength of the hills *is* his also.

5 The sea *is* his, and he made it: and his hands formed the dry *land.*

6 O come, let us worship and bow down: let us kneel before the Lord our maker.

7 For he *is* our God; and we *are* the people of his pasture, and the sheep of his hand. Today if ye will hear his voice,

8 Harden not your heart, as in the provocation, *and* as *in* the day of temptation in the wilderness:

9 When your fathers tempted me, proved me, and saw my work.

10 Forty years long was I grieved with *this* generation, and said, It *is* a people that do err in their heart, and they have not known my ways:

11 Unto whom I sware in my wrath that they should not enter into my rest.

PSALM 97

THE Lord reigneth; let the earth rejoice; let the multitude of isles be glad *thereof.*

2 Clouds and darkness *are* round about him: righteousness and judgment *are* the habitation of his throne.

3 A fire goeth before him, and burneth up his enemies round about.

4 His lightnings enlightened the world: the earth saw, and trembled.

5 The hills melted like wax at the presence of the Lord, at the presence of the Lord of the whole earth.

6 The heavens declare his righteousness, and all the people see his glory.

7 Confounded be all they that serve graven images, that boast themselves of idols: worship him, all *ye* gods.

8 Zion heard, and was glad; and the daughters of Judah rejoiced because of thy judgments, O Lord.

9 For thou, Lord, *art* high above all the earth: thou art exalted far above all gods.

10 Ye that love the Lord, hate evil: he preserveth the souls of his saints; he delivereth them out of the hand of the wicked.

11 Light is sown for the righteous, and gladness for the upright in heart.

12 Rejoice in the Lord, ye righteous; and give thanks at the remembrance of his holiness.

PSALM 103

BLESS the Lord, O my soul: and all that is within me, *bless* his holy name.

2 Bless the Lord, O my soul, and forget not all his benefits:

3 Who forgiveth all thine iniquities; who healeth all thy diseases;

4 Who redeemeth thy life from destruction; who crowneth thee with lovingkindness and tender mercies;

5 Who satisfieth thy mouth with good *things; so that* thy youth is renewed like the eagle's.

6 The Lord executeth righteousness and judgment for all that are oppressed.

7 He made known his ways unto Moses, his acts unto the children of Israel.

8 The Lord *is* merciful and gracious, slow to anger, and plenteous in mercy.

9 He will not always chide: neither will he keep *his anger* for ever.

10 He hath not dealt with us after our sins; nor rewarded us according to our iniquities.

11 For as the heaven is high above the earth, *so* great is his mercy toward them that fear him.

12 As far as the east is from the west, *so* far hath he removed our transgressions from us.

13 Like as a father pitieth *his* children, *so* the Lord pitieth them that fear him.

14 For he knoweth our frame; he remembereth that we *are* dust.

15 *As for* man, his days *are* as grass: as a flower of the field, so he flourisheth.

16 For the wind passeth over it, and it is gone; and the place thereof shall know it no more.

17 But the mercy of the Lord *is* from everlasting to everlasting upon them that fear him, and his righteousness unto children's children;

18 To such as keep his covenant, and to those that remember his commandments to do them.

19 The Lord hath prepared his throne in the heavens; and his kingdom ruleth over all.

20 Bless the Lord, ye his angels, that excel in strength, that do his commandments, hearkening unto the voice of his word.

21 Bless ye the Lord, all *ye* his hosts; *ye* ministers of his, that do his pleasure.

22 Bless the Lord, all his works in all places of his dominion: bless the Lord, O my soul.

PSALM 107

O GIVE thanks unto the Lord, for *he is* good: for his mercy *endureth* for ever.

2 Let the redeemed of the Lord say *so*, whom he hath redeemed from the hand of the enemy;

3 And gathered them out of the lands, from the east, and from the west, from the north, and from the south.

4 They wandered in the wilderness in a solitary way; they found no city to dwell in.

5 Hungry and thirsty, their soul fainted in them.

6 Then they cried unto the Lord in their trouble, *and* he delivered them out of their distresses.

7 And he led them forth by the right way, that they might go to a city of habitation.

8 Oh that *men* would praise the Lord *for* his goodness, and *for* his wonderful works to the children of men!

9 For he satisfieth the longing soul, and filleth the hungry soul with goodness.

10 Such as sit in darkness and in the shadow of death, *being* bound in affliction and iron;

11 Because they rebelled against the words of God, and contemned the counsel of the Most High:

12 Therefore he brought down their heart with labour; they fell down, and *there was* none to help.

13 Then they cried unto the Lord in their trouble, *and* he saved them out of their distresses.

14 He brought them out of darkness and the shadow of death, and brake their bands in sunder.

15 Oh that *men* would praise the Lord *for* his goodness, and *for* his wonderful works to the children of men!

16 For he hath broken the gates of brass, and cut the bars of iron in sunder.

17 Fools because of their transgression, and because of their iniquities, are afflicted.

18 Their soul abhorreth all manner of meat; and they draw

near unto the gates of death.

19 Then they cry unto the LORD in their trouble, *and* he saveth them out of their distresses.

20 He sent his word, and healed them, and delivered *them* from their destructions.

21 Oh that *men* would praise the LORD *for* his goodness, and *for* his wonderful works to the children of men!

22 And let them sacrifice the sacrifices of thanksgiving, and declare his works with rejoicing.

23 They that go down to the sea in ships, that do business in great waters;

24 These see the works of the LORD, and his wonders in the deep.

25 For he commandeth, and raiseth the stormy wind, which lifteth up the waves thereof.

26 They mount up to the heaven, they go down again to the depths: their soul is melted because of trouble.

27 They reel to and fro, and stagger like a drunken man, and are at their wit's end.

28 Then they cry unto the LORD in their trouble, and he bringeth them out of their distresses.

29 He maketh the storm a calm, so that the waves thereof are still.

30 Then are they glad because they be quiet; so he bringeth them unto their desired haven.

31 Oh that *men* would praise the LORD *for* his goodness, and *for* his wonderful works to the children of men!

32 Let them exalt him also in the congregation of the people, and praise him in the assembly of the elders.

33 He turneth rivers into a wilderness, and the watersprings into dry ground;

34 A fruitful land into barrenness, for the wickedness of them that dwell therein.

35 He turneth the wilderness into a standing water, and dry ground into watersprings.

36 And there he maketh the hungry to dwell, that they may prepare a city for habitation;

37 And sow the fields, and plant vineyards, which may yield fruits of increase.

38 He blesseth them also, so that they are multiplied greatly; and suffereth not their cattle to decrease.

39 Again, they are minished and brought low through oppression, affliction, and sorrow.

40 He poureth contempt upon princes, and causeth them to wander in the wilderness, *where there is* no way.

41 Yet setteth he the poor on high from affliction, and maketh *him* families like a flock.

42 The righteous shall see *it*, and rejoice: and all iniquity shall stop her mouth.

43 Whoso *is* wise, and will observe these *things*, even they shall understand the lovingkindness of the LORD.

PSALM 117

O PRAISE the LORD, all ye nations: praise him, all ye people.

2 For his merciful kindness is great toward us: and the truth of the LORD *endureth* for ever. Praise ye the LORD.

PSALMS 146–150

146

PRAISE ye the LORD. Praise the Lord, O my soul.

2 While I live will I praise the LORD: I will sing praises unto my God while I have any being.

3 Put not your trust in princes, *nor* in the son of man, in whom *there is* no help.

4 His breath goeth forth, he returneth to his earth; in that very day his thoughts perish.

5 Happy *is* he that *hath* the God of Jacob for his help, whose hope *is* in the LORD his God:

6 Which made heaven, and earth, the sea, and all that therein *is:* which keepeth truth for ever:

7 Which executeth judgment for the oppressed: which giveth food to the hungry. The LORD looseth the prisoners:

8 The LORD openeth *the eyes of* the blind: the LORD raiseth them that are bowed down: the LORD loveth the righteous:

9 The LORD preserveth the strangers; he relieveth the fatherless and widow: but the way of the wicked he turneth upside down.

10 The LORD shall reign for ever, *even* thy God, O Zion, unto all generations. Praise ye the LORD.

147

PRAISE ye the LORD: for *it is* good to sing praises unto our God; for *it is* pleasant; *and* praise is comely.

2 The LORD doth build up Jerusalem: he gathereth together the outcasts of Israel.

3 He healeth the broken in heart, and bindeth up their wounds.

4 He telleth the number of the stars; he calleth them all by *their* names.

5 Great *is* our Lord, and of great power: his understanding *is* infinite.

6 The LORD lifteth up the meek: he casteth the wicked down to the ground.

7 Sing unto the LORD with thanksgiving; sing praise upon

the harp unto our God:

8 Who covereth the heaven with clouds, who prepareth rain for the earth, who maketh grass to grow upon the mountains.

9 He giveth to the beast his food, *and* to the young ravens which cry.

10 He delighteth not in the strength of the horse: he taketh not pleasure in the legs of a man.

11 The Lord taketh pleasure in them that fear him, in those that hope in his mercy.

12 Praise the Lord, O Jerusalem; praise thy God, O Zion.

13 For he hath strengthened the bars of thy gates; he hath blessed thy children within thee.

14 He maketh peace *in* thy borders, *and* filleth thee with the finest of the wheat.

15 He sendeth forth his commandment *upon* earth: his word runneth very swiftly.

16 He giveth snow like wool: he scattereth the hoarfrost like ashes.

17 He casteth forth his ice like morsels: who can stand before his cold?

18 He sendeth out his word, and melteth them: he causeth his wind to blow, *and* the waters flow.

19 He sheweth his word unto Jacob, his statutes and his judgments unto Israel.

20 He hath not dealt so with any nation: and *as for his* judgments, they have not known them. Praise ye the Lord.

148

PRAISE ye the Lord. Praise ye the Lord from the heavens: praise him in the heights.

2 Praise ye him, all his angels: praise ye him, all his hosts.

3 Praise ye him, sun and moon: praise him, all ye stars of light.

4 Praise him, ye heavens of heavens, and ye waters that *be* above the heavens.

5 Let them praise the name of the Lord: for he commanded, and they were created.

6 He hath also stablished them for ever and ever: he hath made a decree which shall not pass.

7 Praise the Lord from the earth, ye dragons, and all deeps:

8 Fire, and hail; snow, and vapour; stormy wind fulfilling his word:

9 Mountains, and all hills; fruitful trees, and all cedars:

10 Beasts, and all cattle; creeping things, and flying fowl:

11 Kings of the earth, and all people; princes, and all judges of the earth:

12 Both young men, and maidens; old men, and children:

13 Let them praise the name of the Lord: for his name alone is excellent; his glory *is* above the earth and heaven.

14 He also exalteth the horn

of his people, the praise of all his saints; *even* of the children of Israel, a people near unto him. Praise ye the Lord.

149

PRAISE ye the Lord. Sing unto the Lord a new song, *and* his praise in the congregation of saints.

2 Let Israel rejoice in him that made him: let the children of Zion be joyful in their King.

3 Let them praise his name in the dance: let them sing praises unto him with the timbrel and harp.

4 For the Lord taketh pleasure in his people: he will beautify the meek with salvation.

5 Let the saints be joyful in glory: let them sing aloud upon their beds.

6 *Let* the high *praises* of God *be* in their mouth, and a two-edged sword in their hand;

7 To execute vengeance upon the heathen, *and* punishments upon the people;

8 To bind their kings with chains, and their nobles with fetters of iron;

9 To execute upon them the judgment written: this honour have all his saints. Praise ye the Lord.

150

PRAISE ye the Lord. Praise God in his sanctuary: praise him in the firmament of his power.

2 Praise him for his mighty acts: praise him according to his excellent greatness.

3 Praise him with the sound of the trumpet: praise him with the psaltery and harp.

4 Praise him with the timbrel and dance: praise him with stringed instruments and organs.

5 Praise him upon the loud cymbals: praise him upon the high sounding cymbals.

6 Let every thing that hath breath praise the Lord. Praise ye the Lord.

THANKSGIVINGS

PSALM 30

I WILL extoll thee, O Lord; for thou hast lifted me up, and hast not made my foes to rejoice over me.

2 O Lord my God, I cried unto thee, and thou hast healed me.

3 O Lord, thou hast brought up my soul from the grave: thou hast kept me alive, that I should not go down to the pit.

4 Sing unto the Lord, O ye saints of his, and give thanks at the remembrance of his holiness.

5 For his anger *endureth but* a moment; in his favour *is* life: weeping may endure for a night, but joy *cometh* in the morning.

6 And in my prosperity I said, I shall never be moved.

7 Lord, by thy favour thou hast made my mountain to stand strong: thou didst hide thy face, *and* I was troubled.

8 I cried to thee, O Lord; and unto the Lord I made supplication.

9 What profit *is there* in my blood, when I go down to the pit? Shall the dust praise thee? shall it declare thy truth?

10 Hear, O Lord, and have mercy upon me: Lord, be thou my helper.

11 Thou hast turned for me my mourning into dancing: thou hast put off my sackcloth, and girded me with gladness;

12 To the end that *my* glory may sing praise to thee, and not be silent. O Lord my God, I will give thanks unto thee for ever.

PSALM 34

I WILL bless the Lord at all times: his praise *shall* continually *be* in my mouth.

2 My soul shall make her boast in the Lord: the humble shall hear *thereof*, and be glad.

3 O magnify the Lord with me, and let us exalt his name together.

4 I sought the Lord, and he heard me, and delivered me from all my fears.

5 They looked unto him, and were lightened: and their faces were not ashamed.

6 This poor man cried, and the Lord heard *him*, and saved him out of all his troubles.

7 The angel of the Lord encampeth round about them that fear him, and delivereth them.

8 O taste and see that the

L ORD *is* good: blessed *is* the man *that* trusteth in him.

9 O fear the L ORD, ye his saints: for *there is* no want to them that fear him.

10 The young lions do lack, and suffer hunger: but they that seek the L ORD shall not want any good *thing*.

11 Come, ye children, hearken unto me: I will teach you the fear of the L ORD.

12 What man *is he that* desireth life, *and* loveth *many* days, that he may see good?

13 Keep thy tongue from evil, and thy lips from speaking guile.

14 Depart from evil, and do good; seek peace, and pursue it.

15 The eyes of the L ORD *are* upon the righteous, and his ears *are open* unto their cry.

16 The face of the L ORD *is* against them that do evil, to cut off the remembrance of them from the earth.

17 *The righteous* cry, and the L ORD heareth, and delivereth them out of all their troubles.

18 The L ORD *is* nigh unto them that are of a broken heart; and saveth such as be of a contrite spirit.

19 Many *are* the afflictions of the righteous: but the L ORD delivereth him out of them all.

20 He keepeth all his bones: not one of them is broken.

21 Evil shall slay the wicked: and they that hate the righteous shall be desolate.

22 The L ORD redeemeth the soul of his servants: and none of them that trust in him shall be desolate.

PSALM 40, IN PART

I WAITED patiently for the L ORD; and he inclined unto me, and heard my cry.

2 He brought me up also out of an horrible pit, out of the miry clay, and set my feet upon a rock, *and* established my goings.

3 And he hath put a new song in my mouth, *even* praise unto our God: many shall see *it*, and fear, and shall trust in the L ORD.

4 Blessed *is* that man that maketh the L ORD his trust, and respecteth not the proud, nor such as turn aside to lies.

5 Many, O L ORD my God, *are* thy wonderful works *which* thou hast done, and thy thoughts *which are* to us-ward: they cannot be reckoned up in order unto thee: if I would declare and speak *of them*, they are more than can be numbered.

PSALM 116

I LOVE the Lord, because he hath heard my voice *and* my supplications.

2 Because he hath inclined his ear unto me, therefore will I call upon *him* as long as I live.

3 The sorrows of death compassed me, and the pains of hell gat hold upon me: I found trouble and sorrow.

4 Then called I upon the name of the Lord; O Lord, I beseech thee, deliver my soul.

5 Gracious *is* the Lord, and righteous; yea, our God *is* merciful.

6 The Lord preserveth the simple: I was brought low, and he helped me.

7 Return unto thy rest, O my soul; for the Lord hath dealt bountifully with thee.

8 For thou hast delivered my soul from death, mine eyes from tears, *and* my feet from falling.

9 I will walk before the Lord in the land of the living.

10 I believed, therefore have I spoken: I was greatly afflicted:

11 I said in my haste, All men *are* liars.

12 What shall I render unto the Lord *for* all his benefits toward me?

13 I will take the cup of salvation, and call upon the name of the Lord.

14 I will pay my vows unto the Lord now in the presence of all his people.

15 Precious in the sight of the Lord *is* the death of his saints.

16 O Lord, truly I *am* thy servant; I *am* thy servant, *and* the son of thine handmaid: thou hast loosed my bonds.

17 I will offer to thee the sacrifice of thanksgiving, and will call upon the name of the Lord.

18 I will pay my vows unto the Lord now in the presence of all his people,

19 In the courts of the Lord's house, in the midst of thee, O Jerusalem. Praise ye the Lord.

PSALM 118

O GIVE thanks unto the Lord; for *he is* good: because his mercy *endureth* for ever.

2 Let Israel now say, that his mercy *endureth* for ever.

3 Let the house of Aaron now say, that his mercy *endureth* for ever.

4 Let them now that fear the Lord say, that his mercy *endureth* for ever.

5 I called upon the Lord in distress: the Lord answered me, *and set me* in a large place.

6 The Lord *is* on my side; I will not fear: what can man do unto me?

7 The Lord taketh my part with them that help me: therefore shall I see *my desire* upon them that hate me.

8 *It is* better to trust in the Lord than to put confidence in man.

9 *It is* better to trust in the Lord than to put confidence in princes.

10 All nations compassed me about: but in the name of the Lord will I destroy them.

11 They compassed me about; yea, they compassed me about: but in the name of the Lord I will destroy them.

12 They compassed me about like bees; they are quenched as the fire of thorns: for in the name of the Lord I will destroy them.

13 Thou hast thrust sore at me that I might fall: but the Lord helped me.

14 The Lord *is* my strength and song, and is become my salvation.

15 The voice of rejoicing and salvation *is* in the tabernacles of the righteous: the right hand of the Lord doeth valiantly.

16 The right hand of the Lord is exalted: the right hand of the Lord doeth valiantly.

17 I shall not die, but live, and declare the works of the Lord.

18 The Lord hath chastened me sore: but he hath not given me over unto death.

19 Open to me the gates of righteousness: I will go into them, *and* I will praise the Lord:

20 This gate of the Lord, into which the righteous shall enter.

21 I will praise thee: for thou hast heard me, and art become my salvation.

22 The stone *which* the builders refused is become the head *stone* of the corner.

23 This is the Lord's doing; it *is* marvellous in our eyes.

24 This *is* the day *which* the Lord hath made; we will rejoice and be glad in it.

25 Save now, I beseech thee, O Lord: O Lord, I beseech thee, send now prosperity.

26 Blessed *be* he that cometh in the name of the Lord: we have blessed you out of the house of the Lord.

27 God *is* the Lord, which hath shewed us light: bind the sacrifice with cords, *even* unto the horns of the altar.

28 Thou *art* my God, and I will praise thee: *thou art* my God, I will exalt thee.

29 O give thanks unto the Lord; for *he is* good: for his mercy *endureth* for ever.

PSALM 139

O LORD, thou hast searched me, and known *me*.

2 Thou knowest my downsitting and mine uprising, thou understandest my thought afar off.

3 Thou compassest my path and my lying down, and art acquainted *with* all my ways.

4 For *there is* not a word in my tongue, *but*, lo, O LORD, thou knowest it altogether.

5 Thou hast beset me behind and before, and laid thine hand upon me.

6 *Such* knowledge *is* too wonderful for me; it is high, I cannot *attain* unto it.

7 Whither shall I go from thy spirit? or whither shall I flee from thy presence?

8 If I ascend up into heaven, thou *art* there: if I make my bed in hell, behold, thou *art* there.

9 *If* I take the wings of the morning, *and* dwell in the uttermost parts of the sea;

10 Even there shall thy hand lead me, and thy right hand shall hold me.

11 If I say, Surely the darkness shall cover me; even the night shall be light about me.

12 Yea, the darkness hideth not from thee; but the night shineth as the day: the darkness and the light *are* both alike *to* thee.

13 For thou hast possessed my reins: thou hast covered me in my mother's womb.

14 I will praise thee; for I am fearfully *and* wonderfully made: marvellous *are* thy works; and *that* my soul knoweth right well.

15 My substance was not hid from thee, when I was made in secret, *and* curiously wrought in the lowest parts of the earth.

16 Thine eyes did see my substance, yet being unperfect; and in thy book all *my members* were written, *which* in continuance were fashioned, when *as yet there was* none of them.

17 How precious also are thy thoughts unto me, O God! how great is the sum of them!

18 *If* I should count them, they are more in number than the sand: when I awake, I am still with thee.

19 Surely thou wilt slay the wicked, O God: depart from me therefore, ye bloody men.

20 For they speak against thee wickedly, *and* thine enemies take *thy name* in vain.

21 Do not I hate them, O LORD, that hate thee? and am not I grieved with those that rise up against thee?

22 I hate them with perfect

hatred: I count them mine enemies.

23 Search me, O God, and know my heart: try me, and know my thoughts:

24 And see if *there be any* wicked way in me, and lead me in the way everlasting.

LAMENTS

National Laments

WHY standest thou afar off, O LORD? *why* hidest thou *thyself* in times of trouble?

2 The wicked in *his* pride doth persecute the poor: let them be taken in the devices that they have imagined.

3 For the wicked boasteth of his heart's desire, and blesseth the covetous, *whom* the LORD abhorreth.

4 The wicked, through the pride of his countenance, will not seek *after God:* God *is* not in all his thoughts.

5 His ways are always grievous; thy judgments *are* far above out of his sight: *as for* all his enemies, he puffeth at them.

6 He hath said in his heart, I shall not be moved: for *I shall* never *be* in adversity.

7 His mouth is full of cursing and deceit and fraud: under his tongue *is* mischief and vanity.

8 He sitteth in the lurking places of the villages: in the secret places doth he murder the innocent: his eyes are privily set against the poor.

9 He lieth in wait secretly as a lion in his den: he lieth in wait to catch the poor: he doth catch the poor, when he draw-eth him into his net.

10 He croucheth, *and* humbleth himself, that the poor may fall by his strong ones.

11 He hath said in his heart, God hath forgotten: he hideth his face; he will never see *it.*

12 Arise, O LORD; O God, lift up thine hand: forget not the humble.

13 Wherefore doth the wicked contemn God? he hath said in his heart, Thou wilt not require *it.*

14 Thou hast seen *it;* for thou beholdest mischief and spite, to requite *it* with thy hand: the poor committeth himself unto thee; thou art the helper of the fatherless.

15 Break thou the arm of the wicked and the evil *man:* seek out his wickedness *till* thou find none.

16 The LORD *is* King for ever and ever: the heathen are perished out of his land.

17 LORD, thou hast heard the desire of the humble: thou wilt prepare their heart, thou wilt cause thine ear to hear:

18 To judge the fatherless and the oppressed, that the man of the earth may no more oppress.

PSALM 44

WE have heard with our ears, O God, our fathers have told us, *what* work thou didst in their days, in the times of old.

2 *How* thou didst drive out the heathen with thy hand, and plantedst them; *how* thou didst afflict the people, and cast them out.

3 For they got not the land in possession by their own sword, neither did their own arm save them: but thy right hand, and thine arm, and the light of thy countenance, because thou hadst a favour unto them.

4 Thou art my King, O God: command deliverances for Jacob.

5 Through thee will we push down our enemies: through thy name will we tread them under that rise up against us.

6 For I will not trust in my bow, neither shall my sword save me.

7 But thou hast saved us from our enemies, and hast put them to shame that hated us.

8 In God we boast all the day long, and praise thy name for ever. Selah.

9 But thou hast cast off, and put us to shame; and goest not forth with our armies.

10 Thou makest us to turn back from the enemy: and they which hate us spoil for themselves.

11 Thou hast given us like sheep *appointed* for meat; and hast scattered us among the heathen.

12 Thou sellest thy people for nought, and dost not increase *thy wealth* by their price.

13 Thou makest us a reproach to our neighbours, a scorn and a derision to them that are round about us.

14 Thou makest us a byword among the heathen, a shaking of the head among the people.

15 My confusion *is* continually before me, and the shame of my face hath covered me,

16 For the voice of him that reproacheth and blasphemeth; by reason of the enemy and avenger.

17 All this is come upon us; yet have we not forgotten thee, neither have we dealt falsely in thy covenant.

18 Our heart is not turned back, neither have our steps declined from thy way;

19 Though thou hast sore broken us in the place of dragons, and covered us with the shadow of death.

20 If we have forgotten the name of our God, or stretched out our hands to a strange god;

21 Shall not God search this out? for he knoweth the secrets

of the heart.

22 Yea, for thy sake are we killed all the day long; we are counted as sheep for the slaughter.

23 Awake, why sleepest thou, O Lord? arise, cast *us* not off for ever.

24 Wherefore hidest thou thy face, *and* forgettest our affliction and our oppression?

25 For our soul is bowed down to the dust: our belly cleaveth unto the earth.

26 Arise for our help, and redeem us for thy mercies' sake.

PSALM 79

O GOD, the heathen are come into thine inheritance; thy holy temple have they defiled; they have laid Jerusalem on heaps.

2 The dead bodies of thy servants have they given *to be* meat unto the fowls of the heaven, the flesh of thy saints unto the beasts of the earth.

3 Their blood have they shed like water round about Jerusalem; and *there was* none to bury *them*.

4 We are become a reproach to our neighbours, a scorn and derision to them that are round about us.

5 How long, LORD? wilt thou be angry for ever? shall thy jealousy burn like fire?

6 Pour out thy wrath upon the heathen that have not known thee, and upon the kingdoms that have not called upon thy name.

7 For they have devoured Jacob, and laid waste his dwelling place.

8 O remember not against us former iniquities: let thy tender mercies speedily prevent us: for we are brought very low.

9 Help us, O God of our salvation, for the glory of thy name: and deliver us, and purge away our sins, for thy name's sake.

10 Wherefore should the heathen say, Where *is* their God? let him be known among the heathen in our sight *by* the revenging of the blood of thy servants *which is* shed.

11 Let the sighing of the prisoner come before thee; according to the greatness of thy power preserve thou those that are appointed to die;

12 And render unto our neighbours sevenfold into their bosom their reproach, wherewith they have reproached thee, O Lord.

13 So we thy people and sheep of thy pasture will give thee thanks for ever: we will shew forth thy praise to all generations.

Personal Laments

PSALM 6

O LORD, rebuke me not in thine anger, neither chasten me in thy hot displeasure.

2 Have mercy upon me, O LORD; for I *am* weak: O LORD, heal me; for my bones are vexed.

3 My soul is also sore vexed: but thou, O LORD, how long?

4 Return, O LORD, deliver my soul: oh save me for thy mercies' sake.

5 For in death *there is* no remembrance of thee: in the grave who shall give thee thanks?

6 I am weary with my groaning; all the night make I my bed to swim; I water my couch with my tears.

7 Mine eye is consumed because of grief; it waxeth old because of all mine enemies.

8 Depart from me, all ye workers of iniquity; for the LORD hath heard the voice of my weeping.

9 The LORD hath heard my supplication; the LORD will receive my prayer.

10 Let all mine enemies be ashamed and sore vexed: let them return *and* be ashamed suddenly.

PSALM 22

MY God, my God, why hast thou forsaken me? *why art thou so* far from helping me, *and from* the words of my roaring?

2 O my God, I cry in the daytime, but thou hearest not; and in the night season, and am not silent.

3 But thou *art* holy, *O thou* that inhabitest the praises of Israel.

4 Our fathers trusted in thee: they trusted, and thou didst deliver them.

5 They cried unto thee, and were delivered: they trusted in thee, and were not confounded.

6 But I *am* a worm, and no man; a reproach of men, and despised of the people.

7 All they that see me laugh me to scorn: they shoot out the lip, they shake the head, *saying,*

8 He trusted on the LORD *that* he would deliver him: let him deliver him, seeing he delighted in him.

9 But thou *art* he that took me out of the womb: thou didst make me hope *when I was* upon my mother's breasts.

10 I was cast upon thee from

the womb: thou *art* my God from my mother's belly.

11 Be not far from me; for trouble *is* near; for *there is* none to help.

12 Many bulls have compassed me: strong *bulls* of Bashan have beset me round.

13 They gaped upon me *with* their mouths, *as* a ravening and a roaring lion.

14 I am poured out like water, and all my bones are out of joint: my heart is like wax; it is melted in the midst of my bowels.

15 My strength is dried up like a potsherd; and my tongue cleaveth to my jaws; and thou hast brought me into the dust of death.

16 For dogs have compassed me: the assembly of the wicked have inclosed me: they pierced my hands and my feet.

17 I may tell all my bones: they look *and* stare upon me.

18 They part my garments among them, and cast lots upon my vesture.

19 But be not thou far from me, O Lord: O my strength, haste thee to help me.

20 Deliver my soul from the sword; my darling from the power of the dog.

21 Save me from the lion's mouth: for thou hast heard me from the horns of the unicorns.

22 I will declare thy name unto my brethren: in the midst of the congregation will I praise thee.

23 Ye that fear the Lord, praise him; all ye the seed of Jacob, glorify him; and fear him, all ye the seed of Israel.

24 For he hath not despised nor abhorred the affliction of the afflicted; neither hath he hid his face from him; but when he cried unto him, he heard.

25 My praise *shall be* of thee in the great congregation: I will pay my vows before them that fear him.

26 The meek shall eat and be satisfied: they shall praise the Lord that seek him: your heart shall live for ever.

27 All the ends of the world shall remember and turn unto the Lord: and all the kindreds of the nations shall worship before thee.

28 For the kingdom *is* the Lord's: and he *is* the governor among the nations.

29 All *they that be* fat upon earth shall eat and worship: all they that go down to the dust shall bow before him: and none can keep alive his own soul.

30 A seed shall serve him; it shall be accounted to the Lord for a generation.

31 They shall come, and shall declare his righteousness unto a people that shall be born, that he hath done *this*.

PSALM 42-43

AS the hart panteth after the water brooks, so panteth my soul after thee, O God.

2 My soul thirsteth for God, for the living God: when shall I come and appear before God?

3 My tears have been my meat day and night, while they continually say unto me, Where *is* thy God?

4 When I remember these *things*, I pour out my soul in me: for I had gone with the multitude, I went with them to the house of God, with the voice of joy and praise, with a multitude that kept holyday.

5 Why art thou cast down, O my soul? and *why* art thou disquieted in me? hope thou in God: for I shall yet praise him *for* the help of his countenance.

6 O my God, my soul is cast down within me: therefore will I remember thee from the land of Jordan, and of the Hermonites, from the hill Mizar.

7 Deep calleth unto deep at the noise of thy waterspouts; all thy waves and thy billows are gone over me.

8 *Yet* the LORD will command his lovingkindness in the daytime, and in the night his song *shall be* with me, *and* my prayer unto the God of my life.

9 I will say unto God my rock, Why hast thou forgotten me? why go I mourning because of the oppression of the enemy?

10 *As* with a sword in my bones, mine enemies reproach me; while they say daily unto me, Where *is* thy God?

11 Why art thou cast down, O my soul? and why art thou disquieted within me? hope thou in God: for I shall yet praise him, *who is* the health of my countenance, and my God.

12 Judge me, O God, and plead my cause against an ungodly nation: O deliver me from the deceitful and unjust man.

13 For thou *art* the God of my strength: why dost thou cast me off? why go I mourning because of the oppression of the enemy?

14 O send out thy light and thy truth: let them lead me; let them bring me unto thy holy hill, and to thy tabernacles.

15 Then will I go unto the altar of God, unto God my exceeding joy: yea, upon the harp will I praise thee, O God my God.

16 Why art thou cast down, O my soul? and why art thou disquieted within me? hope in God: for I shall yet praise him, *who is* the health of my countenance, and my God.

PSALM 102, IN PART

HEAR my prayer, O Lord, and let my cry come unto thee.

2 Hide not thy face from me in the day *when* I am in trouble; incline thine ear unto me: in the day *when* I call answer me speedily.

3 For my days are consumed like smoke, and my bones are burned as an hearth.

4 My heart is smitten, and withered like grass; so that I forget to eat my bread.

5 By reason of the voice of my groaning my bones cleave to my skin.

6 I am like a pelican of the wilderness: I am like an owl of the desert.

7 I watch, and am as a sparrow alone upon the house top.

8 Mine enemies reproach me all the day; *and* they that are mad against me are sworn against me.

9 For I have eaten ashes like bread, and mingled my drink with weeping,

10 Because of thine indignation and thy wrath: for thou hast lifted me up, and cast me down.

11 My days *are* like a shadow that declineth; and I am withered like grass.

12 But thou, O Lord, shalt endure for ever; and thy remembrance unto all generations.

PSALM 130

OUT of the depths have I cried unto thee, O Lord.

2 Lord, hear my voice: let thine ears be attentive to the voice of my supplications.

3 If thou, Lord, shouldest mark iniquities, O Lord, who shall stand?

4 But *there is* forgiveness with thee, that thou mayest be feared.

5 I wait for the Lord, my soul doth wait, and in his word do I hope.

6 My soul *waiteth* for the Lord more than they that watch for the morning: *I say, more than* they that watch for the morning.

7 Let Israel hope in the Lord: for with the Lord *there is* mercy, and with him *is* plenteous redemption.

8 And he shall redeem Israel from all his iniquities.

HISTORICAL PSALMS

PSALM 46

GOD *is* our refuge and strength, a very present help in trouble.

2 Therefore will not we fear, though the earth be removed, and though the mountains be carried into the midst of the sea;

3 *Though* the waters thereof roar *and* be troubled, *though* the mountains shake with the swelling thereof. Selah.

4 *There is* a river, the streams whereof shall make glad the city of God, the holy *place* of the tabernacles of the most High.

5 God *is* in the midst of her; she shall not be moved: God shall help her, *and that* right early.

6 The heathen raged, the kingdoms were moved: he uttered his voice, the earth melted.

7 The LORD of hosts *is* with us; the God of Jacob *is* our refuge. Selah.

8 Come, behold the works of the LORD, what desolations he hath made in the earth.

9 He maketh wars to cease unto the end of the earth; he breaketh the bow, and cutteth the spear in sunder; he burneth the chariot in the fire.

10 Be still, and know that I *am* God: I will be exalted among the heathen, I will be exalted in the earth.

11 The LORD of hosts *is* with us; the God of Jacob *is* our refuge. Selah.

PSALM 78

GIVE ear, O my people, *to* my law: incline your ears to the words of my mouth.

2 I will open my mouth in a parable: I will utter dark sayings of old:

3 Which we have heard and known, and our fathers have told us.

4 We will not hide *them* from their children, shewing to the generation to come the praises of the LORD, and his strength, and his wonderful works that he hath done.

5 For he established a testimony in Jacob, and appointed a law in Israel, which he commanded our fathers, that they should make them known to their children:

6 That the generation to come might know *them*, *even* the children *which* should be born; *who* should arise and declare *them* to their children:

7 That they might set their hope in God, and not forget the works of God, but keep his commandments:

8 And might not be as their fathers, a stubborn and rebellious generation; a generation *that* set not their heart aright, and whose spirit was not steadfast with God.

9 The children of Ephraim, *being* armed, *and* carrying bows, turned back in the day of battle.

10 They kept not the covenant of God, and refused to walk in his law;

11 And forgat his works, and his wonders that he had shewed them.

12 Marvellous things did he in the sight of their fathers, in the land of Egypt, *in* the field of Zoan.

13 He divided the sea, and caused them to pass through; and he made the waters to stand as an heap.

14 In the daytime also he led them with a cloud, and all the night with a light of fire.

15 He clave the rocks in the wilderness, and gave *them* drink as *out of* the great depths.

16 He brought streams also out of the rock, and caused waters to run down like rivers.

17 And they sinned yet more against him by provoking the Most High in the wilderness.

18 And they tempted God in their heart by asking meat for their lust.

19 Yea, they spake against God; they said, Can God furnish a table in the wilderness?

20 Behold, he smote the rock, that the waters gushed out, and the streams overflowed; can he give bread also? can he provide flesh for his people?

21 Therefore the Lord heard *this,* and was wroth: so a fire was kindled against Jacob, and anger also came up against Israel;

22 Because they believed not in God, and trusted not in his salvation:

23 Though he had commanded the clouds from above, and opened the doors of heaven,

24 And had rained down manna upon them to eat, and had given them of the corn of heaven.

25 Man did eat angels' food: he sent them meat to the full.

26 He caused an east wind to blow in the heaven: and by his power he brought in the south wind.

27 He rained flesh also upon them as dust, and feathered fowls like as the sand of the sea:

28 And he let *it* fall in the midst of their camp, round about their habitations.

29 So they did eat, and were well filled: for he gave them their own desire;

30 They were not estranged from their lust; but while their

meat *was* yet in their mouths,

31 The wrath of God came upon them, and slew the fattest of them, and smote down the chosen *men* of Israel.

32 For all this they sinned still, and believed not for his wondrous works.

33 Therefore their days did he consume in vanity, and their years in trouble.

34 When he slew them, then they sought him: and they returned and enquired early after God.

35 And they remembered that God *was* their rock, and the high God their redeemer.

36 Nevertheless they did flatter him with their mouth, and they lied unto him with their tongues.

37 For their heart was not right with him, neither were they steadfast in his covenant.

38 But he, *being* full of compassion, forgave *their* iniquity, and destroyed *them* not: yea, many a time turned he his anger away, and did not stir up all his wrath.

39 For he remembered that they *were but* flesh; a wind that passeth away, and cometh not again.

40 How oft did they provoke him in the wilderness, *and* grieve him in the desert!

41 Yea, they turned back and tempted God, and limited the Holy One of Israel.

42 They remembered not his hand, *nor* the day when he delivered them from the enemy.

43 How he had wrought his signs in Egypt, and his wonders in the field of Zoan:

44 And had turned their rivers into blood; and their floods, that they could not drink.

45 He sent divers sorts of flies among them, which devoured them; and frogs, which destroyed them.

46 He gave also their increase unto the caterpillar, and their labour unto the locust.

47 He destroyed their vines with hail, and their sycamore trees with frost.

48 He gave up their cattle also to the hail, and their flocks to hot thunderbolts.

49 He cast upon them the fierceness of his anger, wrath, and indignation, and trouble, by sending evil angels *among them.*

50 He made a way to his anger; he spared not their soul from death, but gave their life over to the pestilence;

51 And smote all the firstborn in Egypt; the chief of *their* strength in the tabernacles of Ham:

52 But made his own people to go forth like sheep, and guided them in the wilderness like a flock.

53 And he led them on safely, so that they feared not: but the

sea overwhelmed their enemies.

54 And he brought them to the border of his sanctuary, *even to* this mountain, *which* his right hand had purchased.

55 He cast out the heathen also before them, and divided them an inheritance by line, and made the tribes of Israel to dwell in their tents.

56 Yet they tempted and provoked the most high God, and kept not his testimonies:

57 But turned back, and dealt unfaithfully like their fathers: they were turned aside like a deceitful bow.

58 For they provoked him to anger with their high places, and moved him to jealousy with their graven images.

59 When God heard *this*, he was wroth, and greatly abhorred Israel:

60 So that he forsook the tabernacle of Shiloh, the tent *which* he placed among men;

61 And delivered his strength into captivity, and his glory into the enemy's hand.

62 He gave his people over also unto the sword; and was wroth with his inheritance.

63 The fire consumed their young men; and their maidens were not given to marriage.

64 Their priests fell by the sword; and their widows made no lamentation.

65 Then the Lord awaked as one out of sleep, *and* like a mighty man that shouteth by reason of wine.

66 And he smote his enemies in the hinder parts: he put them to a perpetual reproach.

67 Moreover he refused the tabernacle of Joseph, and chose not the tribe of Ephraim:

68 But chose the tribe of Judah, the mount Zion which he loved.

69 And he built his sanctuary like high *palaces*, like the earth which he hath established for ever.

70 He chose David also his servant, and took him from the sheepfolds:

71 From following the ewes great with young he brought him to feed Jacob his people, and Israel his inheritance.

72 So he fed them according to the integrity of his heart; and guided them by the skillfulness of his hands.

PSALM 105

O GIVE thanks unto the LORD; call upon his name: make known his deeds among the people.

2 Sing unto him, sing psalms unto him: talk ye of all his wondrous works.

3 Glory ye in his holy name: let the heart of them rejoice

that seek the Lord.

4 Seek the Lord, and his strength: seek his face evermore.

5 Remember his marvellous works that he hath done; his wonders, and the judgments of his mouth;

6 O ye seed of Abraham his servant, ye children of Jacob his chosen.

7 He *is* the Lord our God: his judgments *are* in all the earth.

8 He hath remembered his covenant for ever, the word *which* he commanded to a thousand generations.

9 Which *covenant* he made with Abraham, and his oath unto Isaac;

10 And confirmed the same unto Jacob for a law, *and* to Israel *for* an everlasting covenant:

11 Saying, Unto thee will I give the land of Canaan, the lot of your inheritance:

12 When they were *but* a few men in number; yea, very few, and strangers in it.

13 When they went from one nation to another, from *one* kingdom to another people;

14 He suffered no man to do them wrong: yea, he reproved kings for their sakes;

15 *Saying*, Touch not mine anointed, and do my prophets no harm.

16 Moreover he called for a famine upon the land: he brake the whole staff of bread.

17 He sent a man before them, *even* Joseph, *who* was sold for a servant:

18 Whose feet they hurt with fetters: he was laid in iron:

19 Until the time that his word came: the word of the Lord tried him.

20 The king sent and loosed him; *even* the ruler of the people, and let him go free.

21 He made him lord of his house, and ruler of all his substance:

22 To bind his princes at his pleasure; and teach his senators wisdom.

23 Israel also came into Egypt; and Jacob sojourned in the land of Ham.

24 And he increased his people greatly; and made them stronger than their enemies.

25 He turned their heart to hate his people, to deal subtilely with his servants.

26 He sent Moses his servant; *and* Aaron whom he had chosen.

27 They shewed his signs among them, and wonders in the land of Ham.

28 He sent darkness, and made it dark; and they rebelled not against his word.

29 He turned their waters into blood, and slew their fish.

30 Their land brought forth frogs in abundance, in the chambers of their kings.

31 He spake, and there came

divers sorts of flies, *and* lice in all their coasts.

32 He gave them hail for rain, *and* flaming fire in their land.

33 He smote their vines also and their fig trees; and brake the trees of their coasts.

34 He spake, and the locusts came, and caterpillars, and that without number,

35 And did eat up all the herbs in their land, and devoured the fruit of their ground.

36 He smote also all the first-born in their land, the chief of all their strength.

37 He brought them forth also with silver and gold: and *there was* not one feeble *person* among their tribes.

38 Egypt was glad when they departed: for the fear of them fell upon them.

39 He spread a cloud for a covering; and fire to give light in the night.

40 *The people* asked, and he brought quails, and satisfied them with the bread of heaven.

41 He opened the rock, and the waters gushed out; they ran in the dry places *like* a river.

42 For he remembered his holy promise, *and* Abraham his servant.

43 And he brought forth his people with joy, *and* his chosen with gladness:

44 And gave them the lands of the heathen: and they inherited the labour of the people;

45 That they might observe his statutes, and keep his laws. Praise ye the LORD.

PSALM 114

WHEN Israel went out of Egypt, the house of Jacob from a people of strange language;

2 Judah was his sanctuary, *and* Israel his dominion.

3 The sea saw *it*, and fled: Jordan was driven back.

4 The mountains skipped like rams, *and* the little hills like lambs.

5 What *ailed* thee, O thou sea, that thou fleddest? thou

Jordan, *that* thou wast driven back?

6 Ye mountains, *that* ye skipped like rams; *and* ye little hills, like lambs?

7 Tremble, thou earth, at the presence of the Lord, at the presence of the God of Jacob;

8 Which turned the rock *into* a standing water, the flint into a fountain of waters.

PSALM 136

O GIVE thanks unto the LORD; for *he is* good: for his mercy *endureth* for ever.

2 O give thanks unto the God of gods: for his mercy *endureth* for ever.

3 O give thanks to the Lord of lords: for his mercy *endureth* for ever.

4 To him who alone doeth great wonders: for his mercy *endureth* for ever.

5 To him that by wisdom made the heavens: for his mercy *endureth* for ever.

6 To him that stretched out the earth above the waters: for his mercy *endureth* for ever.

7 To him that made great lights: for his mercy *endureth* for ever:

8 The sun to rule by day: for his mercy *endureth* for ever:

9 The moon and stars to rule by night: for his mercy *endureth* for ever.

10 To him that smote Egypt in their firstborn: for his mercy *endureth* for ever:

11 And brought out Israel from among them: for his mercy *endureth* for ever:

12 With a strong hand, and with a stretched out arm: for his mercy *endureth* for ever.

13 To him which divided the Red sea into parts: for his mercy *endureth* for ever:

14 And made Israel to pass through the midst of it: for his mercy *endureth* for ever:

15 But overthrew Pharaoh and his host in the Red sea: for his mercy *endureth* for ever.

16 To him which led his people through the wilderness: for his mercy *endureth* for ever.

17 To him which smote great kings: for his mercy *endureth* for ever:

18 And slew famous kings: for his mercy *endureth* for ever:

19 Sihon king of the Amorites: for his mercy *endureth* for ever:

20 And Og the king of Bashan: for his mercy *endureth* for ever:

21 And gave their land for an heritage: for his mercy *endureth* for ever:

22 *Even* an heritage unto Israel his servant: for his mercy *endureth* for ever.

23 Who remembered us in our low estate: for his mercy *endureth* for ever:

24 And hath redeemed us from our enemies: for his mercy *endureth* for ever.

25 Who giveth food to all flesh: for his mercy *endureth* for ever.

26 O give thanks unto the God of heaven: for his mercy *endureth* for ever.

PSALM 137

BY the rivers of Babylon, there we sat down, yea, we wept, when we remembered Zion.

2 We hanged our harps upon the willows in the midst thereof.

3 For there they that carried us away captive required of us a song; and they that wasted us *required of us* mirth, *saying*, Sing us *one* of the songs of Zion.

4 How shall we sing the Lord's song in a strange land?

5 If I forget thee, O Jerusalem, let my right hand forget *her cunning*.

6 If I do not remember thee, let my tongue cleave to the roof of my mouth; if I prefer not Jerusalem above my chief joy.

7 Remember, O Lord, the children of Edom in the day of Jerusalem; who said, Rase *it*, rase *it*, *even* to the foundation thereof.

8 O daughter of Babylon, who art to be destroyed; happy *shall he be*, that rewardeth thee as thou hast served us.

9 Happy *shall he be*, that taketh and dasheth thy little ones against the stones.

PSALM 145

I WILL extoll thee, my God, O king; and I will bless thy name for ever and ever.

2 Every day will I bless thee; and I will praise thy name for ever and ever.

3 Great *is* the Lord, and greatly to be praised; and his greatness *is* unsearchable.

4 One generation shall praise thy works to another, and shall declare thy mighty acts.

5 I will speak of the glorious honour of thy majesty, and of thy wondrous works.

6 And *men* shall speak of the might of thy terrible acts: and I will declare thy greatness.

7 They shall abundantly utter the memory of thy great goodness, and shall sing of thy righteousness.

8 The Lord *is* gracious, and full of compassion; slow to anger, and of great mercy.

9 The Lord *is* good to all: and his tender mercies *are* over all his works.

10 All thy works shall praise thee, O Lord; and thy saints shall bless thee.

11 They shall speak of the glory of thy kingdom, and talk of thy power;

12 To make known to the sons of men his mighty acts, and the glorious majesty of his kingdom.

13 Thy kingdom *is* an everlasting kingdom, and thy dominion *endureth* throughout all generations.

14 The LORD upholdeth all that fall, and raiseth up all *those that be* bowed down.

15 The eyes of all wait upon thee; and thou givest them their meat in due season.

16 Thou openest thine hand, and satisfiest the desire of every living thing.

17 The LORD *is* righteous in all his ways, and holy in all his works.

18 The LORD *is* nigh unto all them that call upon him, to all that call upon him in truth.

19 He will fulfil the desire of them that fear him: he also will hear their cry, and will save them.

20 The LORD preserveth all them that love him: but all the wicked will he destroy.

21 My mouth shall speak the praise of the LORD: and let all flesh bless his holy name for ever and ever.

PSALMS ABOUT NATURE

PSALM 19:1-6

THE heavens declare the glory of God; and the firmament sheweth his handiwork.

2 Day unto day uttereth speech, and night unto night sheweth knowledge.

3 *There is* no speech nor language, *where* their voice is not heard.

4 Their line is gone out through all the earth, and their words to the end of the world.

In them hath he set a tabernacle for the sun,

5 Which *is* as a bridegroom coming out of his chamber, *and* rejoiceth as a strong man to run a race.

6 His going forth *is* from the end of the heaven, and his circuit unto the ends of it: and there is nothing hid from the heat thereof.

PSALM 29

GIVE unto the Lord, O ye mighty, give unto the Lord glory and strength.

2 Give unto the Lord the glory due unto his name; worship the Lord in the beauty of holiness.

3 The voice of the Lord *is* upon the waters: the God of glory thundereth: the Lord *is* upon many waters.

4 The voice of the Lord *is* powerful; the voice of the Lord *is* full of majesty.

5 The voice of the Lord breaketh the cedars; yea, the Lord breaketh the cedars of Lebanon.

6 He maketh them also to skip like a calf; Lebanon and Sirion like a young unicorn.

7 The voice of the Lord divideth the flames of fire.

8 The voice of the Lord shaketh the wilderness; the Lord shaketh the wilderness of Kadesh.

9 The voice of the Lord maketh the hinds to calve, and discovereth the forests: and in his temple doth every one speak of *his* glory.

10 The Lord sitteth upon the flood; yea, the Lord sitteth King for ever.

11 The Lord will give strength unto his people; the Lord will bless his people with peace.

PSALM 104

BLESS the LORD, O my soul. O LORD my God, thou art very great; thou art clothed with honour and majesty:

2 Who coverest *thyself* with light as *with* a garment; who stretchest out the heavens like a curtain;

3 Who layeth the beams of his chambers in the waters; who maketh the clouds his chariot; who walketh upon the wings of the wind:

4 Who maketh his angels spirits; his ministers a flaming fire:

5 *Who* laid the foundations of the earth, *that* it should not be removed for ever.

6 Thou coveredst it with the deep as *with* a garment: the waters stood above the mountains.

7 At thy rebuke they fled; at the voice of thy thunder they hasted away.

8 They go up by the mountains; they go down by the valleys unto the place which thou hast founded for them.

9 Thou hast set a bound that they may not pass over; that they turn not again to cover the earth.

10 He sendeth the springs into the valleys, *which* run among the hills.

11 They give drink to every beast of the field: the wild asses quench their thirst.

12 By them shall the fowls of the heaven have their habitation, *which* sing among the branches.

13 He watereth the hills from his chambers: the earth is satisfied with the fruit of thy works.

14 He causeth the grass to grow for the cattle, and herb for the service of man: that he may bring forth food out of the earth;

15 And wine *that* maketh glad the heart of man, *and* oil to make *his* face to shine, and bread *which* strengtheneth man's heart.

16 The trees of the LORD are full *of sap;* the cedars of Lebanon, which he hath planted;

17 Where the birds make their nests: *as for* the stork, the fir trees *are* her house.

18 The high hills *are* a refuge for the wild goats; *and* the rocks for the conies.

19 He appointed the moon for seasons: the sun knoweth his going down.

20 Thou makest darkness, and it is night: wherein all the beasts of the forest do creep *forth.*

21 The young lions roar after their prey, and seek their meat from God.

22 The sun ariseth, they gather themselves together, and lay them down in their dens.

23 Man goeth forth unto his work and to his labour until the evening.

24 O Lord, how manifold are thy works! in wisdom hast thou made them all: the earth is full of thy riches.

25 *So is* this great and wide sea, wherein *are* things creeping innumerable, both small and great beasts.

26 There go the ships: *there is* that leviathan, *whom* thou hast made to play therein.

27 These wait all upon thee; that thou mayest give *them* their meat in due season.

28 *That* thou givest them they gather: thou openest thine hand, they are filled with good.

29 Thou hidest thy face, they are troubled: thou takest away their breath, they die, and return to their dust.

30 Thou sendest forth thy spirit, they are created: and thou renewest the face of the earth.

31 The glory of the Lord shall endure for ever: the Lord shall rejoice in his works.

32 He looketh on the earth, and it trembleth: he toucheth the hills, and they smoke.

33 I will sing unto the Lord as long as I live: I will sing praise to my God while I have my being.

34 My meditation of him shall be sweet: I will be glad in the Lord.

35 Let the sinners be consumed out of the earth, and let the wicked be no more. Bless thou the Lord, O my soul. Praise ye the Lord.

PILGRIM SONGS

PSALM 84

HOW amiable *are* thy tabernacles, O Lord of hosts!

2 My soul longeth, yea, even fainteth for the courts of the Lord: my heart and my flesh crieth out for the living God.

3 Yea, the sparrow hath found a house, and the swallow a nest for herself, where she may lay her young, *even* thine altars, O Lord of hosts, my King, and my God.

4 Blessed *are* they that dwell in thy house: they will be still praising thee. Selah.

5 Blessed *is* the man whose strength *is* in thee; in whose heart *are* the ways *of them.*

6 *Who* passing through the valley of Baca make it a well; the rain also filleth the pools.

7 They go from strength to strength, *every one of them* in Zion appeareth before God.

8 O Lord God of hosts, hear my prayer: give ear, O God of Jacob. Selah.

9 Behold, O God our shield, and look upon the face of thine anointed.

10 For a day in thy courts *is* better than a thousand. I had rather be a doorkeeper in the house of my God, than to dwell in the tents of wickedness.

11 For the Lord God *is* a sun and shield: the Lord will give grace and glory: no good *thing* will he withhold from them that walk uprightly.

12 O Lord of hosts, blessed *is* the man that trusteth in thee.

PSALM 121

I WILL lift up mine eyes unto the hills, from whence cometh my help.

2 My help *cometh* from the Lord, which made heaven and earth.

3 He will not suffer thy foot to be moved: he that keepeth thee will not slumber.

4 Behold, he that keepeth Israel shall neither slumber nor sleep.

5 The Lord *is* thy keeper: the Lord *is* thy shade upon thy right hand.

6 The sun shall not smite thee by day, nor the moon by night.

7 The Lord shall preserve thee from all evil: he shall preserve thy soul.

8 The Lord shall preserve thy going out and thy coming in from this time forth, and even for evermore.

PSALM 122

I WAS glad when they said unto me, Let us go into the house of the Lord.

2 Our feet shall stand within thy gates, O Jerusalem.

3 Jerusalem is builded as a city that is compact together:

4 Whither the tribes go up, the tribes of the Lord, unto the testimony of Israel, to give thanks unto the name of the Lord.

5 For there are set thrones of judgment, the thrones of the house of David.

6 Pray for the peace of Jerusalem: they shall prosper that love thee.

7 Peace be within thy walls, *and* prosperity within thy palaces.

8 For my brethren and companions' sakes, I will now say, Peace *be* within thee.

9 Because of the house of the Lord our God I will seek thy good.

PSALM 125

THEY that trust in the Lord *shall be* as mount Zion, *which* cannot be removed, *but* abideth for ever.

2 *As* the mountains *are* round about Jerusalem, so the Lord *is* round about his people from henceforth even for ever.

3 For the rod of the wicked shall not rest upon the lot of the righteous; lest the righteous put forth their hands unto iniquity.

4 Do good, O Lord, unto *those that be* good, and to *them that are* upright in their hearts.

5 As for such as turn aside unto their crooked ways, the Lord shall lead them forth with the workers of iniquity: *but* peace *shall be* upon Israel.

PSALM 126

WHEN the Lord turned again the captivity of Zion, we were like them that dream.

2 Then was our mouth filled with laughter, and our tongue with singing: then said they among the heathen, The Lord hath done great things for them.

3 The Lord hath done great things for us; *whereof* we are glad.

4 Turn again our captivity, O

LORD, as the streams in the south.

5 They that sow in tears shall reap in joy.

6 He that goeth forth and weepeth, bearing precious seed, shall doubtless come again with rejoicing, bringing his sheaves *with him.*

PSALMS OF PERSONAL
MEDITATION AND
REFLECTION

PSALM 23

THE Lord *is* my shepherd; I shall not want.

2 He maketh me to lie down in green pastures: he leadeth me beside the still waters.

3 He restoreth my soul: he leadeth me in the paths of righteousness for his name's sake.

4 Yea, though I walk through the valley of the shadow of death, I will fear no evil: for thou *art* with me; thy rod and thy staff they comfort me.

5 Thou preparest a table before me in the presence of mine enemies: thou anointest my head with oil; my cup runneth over.

6 Surely goodness and mercy shall follow me all the days of my life: and I will dwell in the house of the Lord for ever.

PSALM 27

THE Lord *is* my light and my salvation; whom shall I fear? the Lord *is* the strength of my life; of whom shall I be afraid?

2 When the wicked, *even* mine enemies and my foes, came upon me to eat up my flesh, they stumbled and fell.

3 Though an host should encamp against me, my heart shall not fear: though war should rise against me, in this *will* I *be* confident.

4 One *thing* have I desired of the Lord, that will I seek after; that I may dwell in the house of the Lord all the days of my life, to behold the beauty of the Lord, and to inquire in his temple.

5 For in the time of trouble he shall hide me in his pavilion: in the secret of his tabernacle shall he hide me; he shall set me up upon a rock.

6 And now shall mine head be lifted up above mine enemies round about me: therefore will I offer in his tabernacle sacrifices of joy; I will sing, yea, I will sing praises unto the Lord.

7 Hear, O Lord, *when* I cry with my voice: have mercy also upon me, and answer me.

8 *When thou saidst,* Seek ye my face; my heart said unto thee, Thy face, Lord, will I seek.

9 Hide not thy face *far* from me; put not thy servant away

in anger: thou hast been my help; leave me not, neither forsake me, O God of my salvation.

10 When my father and my mother forsake me, then the Lord will take me up.

11 Teach me thy way, O Lord, and lead me in a plain path, because of mine enemies.

12 Deliver me not over unto the will of mine enemies: for false witnesses are risen up against me, and such as breathe out cruelty.

13 *I had fainted*, unless I had believed to see the goodness of the Lord in the land of the living.

14 Wait on the Lord: be of good courage, and he shall strengthen thine heart: wait, I say, on the Lord.

PSALM 90

LORD, thou hast been our dwelling place in all generations.

2 Before the mountains were brought forth, or ever thou hadst formed the earth and the world, even from everlasting to everlasting, thou *art* God.

3 Thou turnest man to destruction; and sayest, Return, ye children of men.

4 For a thousand years in thy sight *are but* as yesterday when it is past, and *as* a watch in the night.

5 Thou carriest them away as with a flood; they are *as* a sleep: in the morning *they are* like grass *which* groweth up.

6 In the morning it flourisheth, and groweth up; in the evening it is cut down, and withereth.

7 For we are consumed by thine anger, and by thy wrath are we troubled.

8 Thou hast set our iniquities before thee, our secret *sins* in the light of thy countenance.

9 For all our days are passed away in thy wrath: we spend our years as a tale *that is told*.

10 The days of our years *are* threescore years and ten; and if by reason of strength *they be* fourscore years, yet *is* their strength labour and sorrow; for it is soon cut off, and we fly away.

11 Who knoweth the power of thine anger? even according to thy fear, *so is* thy wrath.

12 So teach *us* to number our days, that we may apply *our* hearts unto wisdom.

13 Return, O Lord, how long? and let it repent thee concerning thy servants.

14 O satisfy us early with thy mercy; that we may rejoice and be glad all our days.

15 Make us glad according to the days *wherein* thou hast af-

flicted us, *and* the years *where-in* we have seen evil.

16 Let thy work appear unto thy servants, and thy glory unto their children.

17 And let the beauty of the Lord our God be upon us: and establish thou the work of our hands upon us; yea, the work of our hands establish thou it.

PSALM 91

HE that dwelleth in the secret place of the most High shall abide under the shadow of the Almighty.

2 I will say of the Lord, *He is* my refuge and my fortress: my God; in him will I trust.

3 Surely he shall deliver thee from the snare of the fowler, *and* from the noisome pestilence.

4 He shall cover thee with his feathers, and under his wings shalt thou trust: his truth *shall be thy* shield and buckler.

5 Thou shalt not be afraid for the terror by night; *nor* for the arrow *that* flieth by day;

6 *Nor* for the pestilence *that* walketh in darkness; *nor* for the destruction *that* wasteth at noonday.

7 A thousand shall fall at thy side, and ten thousand at thy right hand; *but* it shall not come nigh thee.

8 Only with thine eyes shalt thou behold and see the reward of the wicked.

9 Because thou hast made the Lord, *which is* my refuge, *even* the Most High, thy habitation;

10 There shall no evil befall thee, neither shall any plague come nigh thy dwelling.

11 For he shall give his angels charge over thee, to keep thee in all thy ways.

12 They shall bear thee up in *their* hands, lest thou dash thy foot against a stone.

13 Thou shalt tread upon the lion and adder: the young lion and the dragon shalt thou trample under feet.

14 Because he hath set his love upon me, therefore will I deliver him: I will set him on high, because he hath known my name.

15 He shall call upon me, and I will answer him: I *will be* with him in trouble: I will deliver him, and honour him.

16 With long life will I satisfy him, and shew him my salvation.

2

A Short Account of the History of Israel

1. The Age of the Patriarchs

NO ONE with even a slight knowledge of the Old Testament could have failed to be deeply moved when in May, 1948, the new State of Israel, *Eretz Israel* (in Hebrew, the land of Israel) came into being; and to those familiar with the long and often bitter and tragic history of the Hebrews as a people this emotion was a most profound one. All who have for years been devoted students of this ancient land, its history, its life, and its literature, rejoiced in the words of the Psalms "with exceeding joy."

The distant beginnings of the actual history of Israel as a people and as a nation are hidden in tradition and legend. When we read the fascinating stories in Genesis, stories which after the legends of the Creation and the Flood, center from Genesis 12 to 50 about the figures of Abraham, Isaac, Jacob, and Joseph, we must always remember that this great family saga, one of the very greatest in any literature and written by most gifted narrators, took literary form almost a thousand years after the events themselves together with the persons involved in them are said to have had their being. Their authors received such stories from the oral traditions current in their own day. What sturdy reliance, then, can we place upon their masterly accounts?

Abraham, Isaac, and Jacob are known as the patriarchs, or as the "fathers" of Israel, and their age is called the patriarchal age. Throughout the Old Testament they are held to be the remote ancestors of the Hebrews and even to have worshiped in those faraway ages the one God of the Hebrew people as He later revealed Himself to Moses. How true are these stories? What solid dependence can we place upon them in terms of sober history?

These questions are impossible to answer with any promise of exact truth. Genesis is our sole literary source for the patriarchs. Everything depends, of course, upon the accuracy with which their stories were told from one generation to another over the course of almost ten long centuries. Were they carefully treasured and transmitted without additions and without tempting embroidery? All know how easy it is for a dramatic story-teller to enhance his narrative by bits of his own imagination; and yet all know, too, how carefully and tenaciously family lore and customs can be, and often are, cherished and preserved. Moreover, care and tenacity might well be especially characteristic of the ancient Hebrews, who, perhaps more than any other people, felt a religious obligation to preserve their background intact and true, at least in its main aspects.

A half century ago many, if not most of the best scholars were convinced that the patriarchs were legendary rather than historical figures; but today they have become equally convinced that there are more authentic details in the Genesis account of them than were once thought likely. This latter conclusion arises from fairly recent archaeological discoveries, dating back to the fifteenth century B.C., discoveries which, in the form of documents deciphered from clay tablets found in Assyria, prove that the social customs described in Genesis are remarkably accurate accounts of ways and manners prevailing during the time of Abraham in what we know today as the Near East. And if social customs, such, for example, as the sale of a birthright, so vividly told in Genesis 25; a death-bed blessing, which Jacob gave to his sons in Genesis 49; and the valued possession of family idols, or household gods, which Rachel, we remember, stole from her father, Laban, when she started back to his home with her husband, Jacob, then what more natural than to assume that people like Esau, Jacob, and Rachel, if perhaps not called by their identical names, lived by such customs in their family lives?

When then did these patriarchs of Israel live? Where did they come from? Probably they lived in the second millennium B.C., or, to take a chance on more exact dates, around the years 1750 to 1600. Such centuries seem very far away until we remember that the world was already old when Abraham, Isaac, and Jacob, who were perhaps not grandfather, father, and son but, instead, separated by several generations, or who might well have been the leaders of separate Hebrew clans, drifted into Syria and south to Canaan, or Palestine. Great kingdoms, like that of ancient Sumeria in the valley of the Tigris and Euphrates, the first great empire of ancient times, and like that of Egypt, had already flourished a thousand years before Abraham's day.

There were peoples eager for invasion and conquest, such as the Hittites of Asia Minor, who two centuries before the time of Abraham had built one empire and were later to build yet another. There were Hurrians, and Amorites, and Arameans, and many lesser tribes and clans, all bent upon finding lands better than those from which they had come. Many though not all of these peoples were of Semitic stock like the Hebrews, who may be thought of as a relatively small tribe of that vast race.

To wander into other lands was clearly an indigenous quality of the ancient Semites. From 3000 to 1000 B.C. these people, or peoples, migrated in great waves into the fertile valleys of the Tigris and the Euphrates rivers and into adjacent lands as well. The patriarchs of Israel were, it is quite safe to assume, among these wanderers and invaders from the desert lands to the south. They were nomadic, or semi-nomadic, by nature, living in tents, tending their flocks of sheep and goats, and moving from place to place in search of grass and water. The more energetic and powerful among them were bent on conquest, on new civilizations of their own; the lesser clans and tribes were not so ambitious. The tradition which tells us that Abraham himself came from the old city-state of Ur of the Chaldees may well be true since these Semitic folk had been long known as invaders of the Mesopotamian region.

Wherever Abraham came from, he surely did not belong to any barren or uninhabited world. In his day there was constant interchange of culture and trade among various kingdoms, empires, or city-states. Nations waxed strong and waned; kingdoms and empires knew both prosperity and strength as well as poverty and weakness. Nor must we think that migrations and invasions necessarily destroyed or displaced the former inhabitants of any area. It is far more reasonable to think that the newcomers mingled with the people among whom they came, intermarrying with them and assimilating aspects and features of their new life and environment. The Old Testament narratives tell us often how enticing were the various religious cults which the ancient Hebrews discovered among their new neighbours, and how many of them embraced such cults. And if religious practices, surely social customs and ways of life as well. We know, for example, that their language was closely allied to that of the Canaanites among whom they settled, which fact may suggest that they either abandoned their own or took over so many Canaanitish forms that the language through the centuries finally became one and the same.

What then shall we conclude about these patriarchal figures, whose stories equal or surpass the tales of the Greeks,—the Trojan War, Helen, whose face was so lovely that it "launched a thousand ships," Agamemnon, Achilles, Hecuba, Cassandra? These Grecian and Trojan legends are so familiar that they have become true to us; and in the past decades history has concluded that there is far more truth in them than it heretofore had been willing to concede. The stories in Genesis have for centuries taken on themselves the same *real*, if not *absolute*, values. Shall we not, then, safely assume that there were nearly four thousand years ago actual individuals named Abraham, Isaac, and Jacob, who, having journeyed from the east or from the southern deserts, lived in what we now know as Syria and Palestine, and that it is very possible they were the heads of separate Semitic clans or tribes which eventually came together to form the

Biblical Hebrews? Perhaps Abraham headed the southern clans, and Jacob the northern. Perhaps again the tribe of Jacob, who, we remember, was given the name of *Israel* after wrestling with the angel, came to be even more important than that of Abraham, the traditional father of the Hebrew people.

And what shall we conclude about their religion? Did they actually worship that "God of the Fathers" as the Old Testament and the New Testament declare in so many passages and as the psalmists also assert in several of their poems? About this worship we have no sure evidence; and yet we do possess several statements in the Exodus narratives that the God who is revealing Himself to Moses is the Lord God of the fathers, "the God of Abraham, the God of Isaac, and the God of Jacob." It would seem at least unlikely that such a fervent tradition of religious faith is wholly without foundation in fact, or that Moses, when he inspired his people to flee from oppression in Egypt, was appealing to them in the name of a faith of which they had no inheritance and knowledge.

Perhaps we are safest when we assume that the patriarchs of Israel, both in their earliest wanderings into Canaan and in their life there and in the later centuries when certain of their descendants fled to Egypt for food and water for themselves and their flocks, must have adhered to some form of religion which bore within it the seeds of the Mosaic faith; that it possessed a sense of the close relationship between God and man; that it recognized God's concern for men, as well as His demands for righteousness, justice, and mercy. Surely such qualities, so inherent in the extraordinary and beautiful stories of Genesis, almost compel one to believe that these stories, though perhaps not true in all

details, are nevertheless grounded upon facts carefully preserved and as carefully handed down from generation to
generation.

2. The Age of the Exodus and the Settlement in Canaan

The book of Exodus deals, of course, with the Exodus itself, that greatest single event in the long history of Israel.
Its chief character is Moses, who led his people in their
escape from the oppression of the Pharaoh of Egypt, probably Ramses II,—an escape which, as generally agreed upon
by the best scholars, took place in the thirteenth century
B.C., around the year 1250. Exodus, like Genesis, is not by
any means free of legends, in which, in fact, it abounds. We
must always remember, however, that legends inevitably
occur whenever and wherever extraordinary individuals
appear in history, whether such tales have to do with a
cherry tree, or a rock in Plymouth, with a baby in a basket,
or a succession of monstrous plagues, or a rod changing
into a serpent. Thus legends are, in a very real sense, a
natural accretion to history simply because outstanding and
remarkable people give rise always to stories which may
well not be literally true, but which nevertheless serve to
characterize those around whom they cluster.

Exodus is not so easy a book to read as is Genesis, partly
because so many authors had a hand in its composition over
at least three or four centuries, largely because in its compilation, made around 400 B.C., together with the rest of
the Pentateuch or "Five Books of Moses," and long after
most of it was written, its editors allowed so much discursive
material to dim the actual figure of Moses. It will be our job

here to try to extract him from legends and from numberless rites and laws and to see what manner of man he was.
Without doubt he gave the most priceless contribution to
the social, religious, and political history of his people and
was held through successive centuries, as he is, indeed, held
today, to be not only their saviour from tyranny, but the
founder of their nation and the revealer of their faith.

In one outstanding particular the book of Exodus is
clearly different from Genesis. The stories in Genesis have
to do with family life, with people in common, familiar relationships, noble and ignoble, good and evil. Those in Exodus
deal, instead, with Hebrew tribes, conscious of their tribal
relationships and already beginning to see themselves as a
people and even as a nation. This consciousness can be attributed largely to Moses himself, to his consummate genius
both as a most practical leader of men and as an inspired
religious teacher.

Whether or not Moses was set afloat by his frightened
mother in a basket among the bulrushes of the Nile and
found by an Egyptian princess who brought him up, does
not really matter in terms of actual fact. What does matter
is his stature as a man and his almost incredible services to
Israel. Without much doubt he was born in Egypt and
brought up there, although he was apparently never unaware of his Hebrew inheritance. At some time in his young
manhood he became distressed over the condition of certain
Hebrew tribes who, perhaps some centuries earlier, had
migrated to Egypt where they, in common, with other
Semitic peoples, had been allowed to make their homes on
Egyptian frontiers. They supposedly were living in Goshen
near the mouth of the Nile and in the thirteenth century
had for some years been compelled by the Egyptian king to

labour on certain ambitious building programs of his near or in the ancient cities of Pithom and Ramses in the Goshen region.

Moses, we are told, because of his fury over their oppression, one day killed an Egyptian taskmaster, who was abusing a Hebrew workman, and was obliged to flee for his life into the wilderness of Midian where he took refuge with a Semitic tribe known as the Kenites, who lived in the desert region south of Canaan, an area now known as the Negev. Here he met Jethro, or Reuel, as he is also called, the priest of the Kenites, and later married his daughter. These Kenites were worshipers of one God, known as Yahveh, or the Lord God. Moses learned from them of this God, who, he became convinced, was the selfsame God of the patriarchs of his people, and to whom, probably under Jethro's influence, he dedicated himself anew.

This flaming faith of Moses, doubtless composed of features both old and new, brought him back under the command of God to his suffering kinsmen in Egypt. He persuaded them that their ancient tribal God whom their forefathers had worshiped, had a special care and concern for them as a people and as a future nation. In other words, his first and perhaps greatest gift to these kinsmen was to inspire them with a flaming sense of national unity, always deeply religious in character. Whether he *re-made* their faith, *re-newed* it, *re-activated* it, *re-formed* it, *re-established* it, history does not clearly tell us; yet the entire Old Testament bears witness, in its legend, its tradition, *and* its history, that his labour in behalf of his people was the solid basis of their life as a nation.

Such a fact as this should set aside as unimportant any questions we may have concerning the literal truth of much of the story of Moses. He was, we must never forget, a man of his own time. That the God of his fathers was a mountain God who spoke in thunders and lightnings, as did the God of Psalm 29, that He could send plagues against the Egyptians, "harden the heart" of the perplexed and desperate Pharaoh, and at times threaten His "stiff-necked people" with destruction,—all these conceptions of Deity were the conceptions of his age and place. The amazing quality in Moses was that he was able to discern behind all these primitive aspects of God, the truth of His justice and righteousness, the ethical and spiritual demands which He makes of men, and the entire loyalty which He requires of them. To Moses the awesomeness of God, whether seen in a smoking mountain or a burning bush, was only a part of His Reality. By far the greater part lay in His closeness to men and in His partnership with them. Moses has justly been called the first of the Hebrew prophets because, five centuries before the time of the great prophets, he defined, largely in their own terms, what was to him the true nature of God.

How many people fled from Goshen with Moses as their leader, we do not know. Probably only a few thousand, perhaps five thousand at most, since the wilderness could not have supported the much exaggerated figures given in the Old Testament. And other exaggerations and inconsistencies without doubt occur in the story of their escape. They did not, for example, cross the Red Sea, but, instead, the "Sea of Reeds," which could correctly describe any part of a region of small lakes and marshes along the eastern frontier of Egypt. Nor did the Pharaoh, who, in the face of severe catastrophes overwhelming his land and known in tradition as *plagues*, finally permitted these Hebrews to go

"a three days journey into the wilderness" to sacrifice to
their God, probably send his entire army either to compel
them to return or to destroy them. We are on far safer
ground when we discern through the mist of legendary material the fact that under the leadership of Moses they
crossed the inhospitable, watery ground east of Goshen,
perhaps assisted by weather favourable to them, whereas the
"hosts of Pharaoh" were destroyed in their pursuit.

Nor can we exactly know just where Moses led them,
but probably some 150 miles east from Goshen through the
wilderness to a place called Kadesh-Barnea, near Mount
Sinai, or Horeb. Here there seems to have been a more or
less stable community of Semitic tribes, among whom were
the Kenites, who held as one of their holy places the springs
in the vicinity of Kadesh and the sacred mountain. Neither
can we be sure that these forty years in the wilderness are
any exact space of time, since "forty years" is a term far
more popular than precise throughout the entire Old Testament.

What we can be sure of through the force of a dynamic
faith, persisting for over one thousand years of Old Testament history and still active and invulnerable among Jewish
people today, is the Covenant made in this wilderness between God and His newly chosen people, chosen not because of their *superiority* over others, but because of their
faith, their inherent *strength*, both physical and spiritual,
and their sense of *responsibility*. This ancient idea of covenant is not only firmly rooted in the compact, the agreement
between God and Israel which followed the deliverance
from Egyptian bondage. It was also fundamental to closely
knit Semitic groups as we read again and again in the Old
Testament. Jacob made a covenant with God after his

dream at Bethel and set up a stone to mark that sacred place and the promises which he and God exchanged there, as we read in Genesis 28. In Genesis 31 Laban and Jacob made a covenant, also marked by a stone pillar. Joshua, the successor of Moses (who died before the Israelites entered Canaan), made a covenant, again with a commemorative pillar, to merge under the leadership of God the Hebrews of the Exodus with the Hebrew clans already in Canaan. Two centuries later David and Jonathan made a covenant of friendship; and still later King Ahab made a covenant with the king of Syria.

A covenant, then, lay deep in Hebrew life and ways. It meant a solemn promise by which men established their mutual dependence upon one another or by which they openly confirmed their pledge of fealty either to other men or to God. It symbolized reciprocity, inter-relationship, participation, companionship. The handshake in its earliest beginnings signified a covenant. Grace before meals, the breaking of bread, the Jewish Passover, the Christian Eucharist—all these have their sources in the ancient idea of covenant.

Just what the Sacred Covenant in the wilderness of Kadesh was in its simplest form we do not know, since many later laws, observances, and sacrifices have been added to it; but that it took place there was never any doubt in the devout Hebraic mind and heart. By its terms, as given by God to Moses, God in return and in exchange for the complete loyalty and devotion of His people promises that He will be with them in all their ways, that He will battle with them against their enemies, and that He will give them a land for their settlement, the Promised Land, the Land of Canaan.

The word *settlement* is, for several reasons, a far more accurate term than is *conquest* to describe the entrance into Canaan of the Hebrew tribes from the wilderness of Kadesh. In the first place, many clans closely related to them had been in Canaan for centuries, not having gone down into Egypt. In the second place, there was apparently at least a *relatively* peaceful co-existence between the newcomers and the natives of Canaan. In the third place, the settlement did not so much mean actual warfare, except in the battle so vividly described in Judges 5 between the Canaanites under Sisera and the Israelites under Deborah and Barak, as it meant a continuous amalgamation of Semitic peoples, one the Canaanites, a pastoral, long-settled folk, the other, the people of Moses and of God from the wilderness. And finally the entrance into Canaan and settlement there was probably a matter of almost two centuries, carried out by various tribes and clans, roughly from 1200 B.C. until the beginning of Israel as a kingdom not far from 1020 B.C.

Probably such settlement was gradual, the invaders coming at first into the hills of the country, which, we must remember, was small, about the size of our state of Vermont. The Canaanites held the plains and the trade routes leading to other lands; and they possessed weapons and other armed strength unknown to the invading Israelites. Military action was without doubt needed to take certain parts of Canaan, as Deborah's ode bears witness; yet it would be inaccurate to assume that all the inhabitants were actively hostile to the newcomers, especially since many of them were closely related to the Children of Israel. What surely was different between the plain and the hill dwellers, or between the Canaanites and the invaders, was the Mosaic faith in God which marked the newcomers and which was eventually to spread its strength and its influence throughout the land just as the Canaanitish language was in the end to prove stronger than that of the new settlers and make one tongue, known as *Hebrew*.

If one quite naturally asks why the Israelites of all the many tribes represented in Canaan should prove to be the most powerful, the answer probably lies partly at least in the free, resilient, independent, proud spirit, characteristic of nomadic peoples, but largely in the power of the Mosaic faith and in the sturdy reliance upon the promises of God, a faith and a reliance which produced a remarkable sense of unity. There were without doubt many threatening and disintegrating forces both from the agricultural character of Canaan, unfamiliar and at first distasteful to desert dwellers and to nomadic shepherds, and from the strong appeal of Canaanitish Baal worship; yet though, as the Old Testament assures us, there were many instances of apostasy from the faith of Israel, it obviously held its own against the sensual nature cults of the Canaanites. Fade and flicker though it might, and unquestionably did, it inevitably flared into life again when any danger or crisis arose, and resulted finally in the political, social, and religious mastery of the Israelitish clans.

Without doubt, too, the power of Israel was vastly increased, if not largely assured, by the appearance in Canaan, about a century after the arrival of the Hebrew tribes, of non-Semitic peoples known as Philistines, who, coming from islands in the Aegean, seemed bent on conquest of the Near Eastern world. Repulsed in Egypt, they came in hordes northward and began to settle down on the southern coastal plain of Canaan above the Mediterranean. Their early-Greek civilization was hateful to both Canaanites and Israelites alike; and they drew together as one Semitic people to repeal the advances of these aliens, whose superiority in arms and in military organization made them a dangerous and a common enemy. Now the invading Hebrew tribes were not so much defeating the Canaanites as defending them against a threatening foe. This incursion of the Philistines, who quickly over-ran the coastal plain and built five flourishing cities, Gath, Gaza, Askelon, Ashdod, and Ekron, surely resulted in a unity of purpose and action which otherwise might have been postponed for many years.

During the two centuries of gradual occupation and settlement of the Israelite tribes in Canaan, the basic unit of social life among them continued to be tribal, the most powerful of the tribes assuming the overlordship of the weaker. "In those days," the book of Judges tells us in its final verse, "there was no king in Israel: every man did that which was right in his own eyes." Such leaders of the dominant tribes were known as *judges,* probably, at least in its modern connotation, an inappropriate term, since the Biblical judges were in no sense magistrates, but, rather, especially endowed religious leaders, often of an almost fanatical cast, as the stories in the book of Judges bear witness. They were apparently not elected or chosen, but "arose," in the words of Deborah, and took leadership. The stories of them which make Judges such a fascinating book to read and which are of inestimable value for their portrayal of life and customs in the twelfth and eleventh centuries, B.C., were probably at first separate accounts and later assembled to form the book as a whole.

Perhaps the statement that "every man did that which was right in his own eyes" suggests a rather idealistic picture of life in a primitive, turbulent, and barbaric age. Some of the judges like Gideon and Jephthah fought in the name of God against neighbouring peoples bent on marauding and invasion, the Midianites and the Ammonites. Samson claimed to be a judge; but he was probably a kind of folk hero, instead, whose guerrilla warfare against the Philistines was without doubt commendable, but whose love affairs were hardly admirable. Ehud seemed more gifted at murder than at religious leadership, his treacherous stabbing of Eglon, king of Moab, exceeded only by the wholesale murder of his own brothers by the traitorous Abimelech, son of Gideon. And the enigmatic Samuel, the last of the judges and the most important of them, seems, in his chaotically assembled chronicle in which many contrasting stories vie for truth, to have been harsh and cruel as well as wise and faithful.

Yet in this age of barbarism and disregard of human life there were happier, less sorry features. We must not forget that the idyllic and charming story of Ruth took place "in the days when the judges ruled"; or that Gideon when, in recognition of his bravery, he was asked to reign as king, stoutly refused, saying that only God could rightly rule a people dedicated to Him. The amazing feature of the age, in fact, is not its barbarism, but rather the wonder that the religion of Moses could and did not only endure, but survive all its corruption and cruelty. For the Holy Covenant made in the wilderness was clearly not forgotten even in the midst of a hostile and backsliding world. And the Israelites, as with the tribes in Canaan closely related to them they continued to possess the land, partly by mingling with the Canaanites, partly through defense against a common enemy, and always by their faith in the promises of God,

found themselves after two centuries a nation ready for a
more stable history.

3. The Age of the United Kingdom

The one hundred years of the united kingdom of Israel,
from around 1020 B.C. to the year 922, marked the reigns
of three kings, Saul, David, and Solomon. They marked,
too, the final domination of Canaan by the tribes of Israel;
the conquest of the Philistines; and the coming of age of
Israel as a really important, if small, nation. Much of its
power was due without doubt to the weakened condition
of the great kingdoms and empires to the south and east,
notably those of Egypt and Assyria, both of which were
concerned with internal affairs and neither of which at the
time possessed able rulers. The Israelites, always ready to
seize upon any situation advantageous to them, prospered
in proportion as their greater, more powerful neighbours
declined in strength.

Their three kings, all men of ability and determination,
came into being because of the desire of Israel for a monarchy. Saul won his throne, always uncongenial to him, by
popular choice; David by conquest; Solomon by inheritance.
A king, we are told in the book of I Samuel, seemed a neces-
sity in order that more successful war might be waged
against the still encroaching Philistines. Moreover, kings
were the usual rulers of the time, whether of empires, kingdoms, or cities. Each Philistine city had its *seren*, its tyrant
or king; and Israel, once it had made itself supreme in
Canaan, was eager to follow the monarchial custom of its
day. Saul was apparently the last of the judges as well as the
first of the kings of Israel.

The tragic and noble story of King Saul, as told in I
Samuel, shows him to have been a man of simple tastes and
of great religious zeal, a member of the small Israelite tribe
of Benjamin. He held as his stronghold the provincial town
of Gibeah, where he built a fortress, but no kingly palace.
He was not a young man when he ascended the new throne
of Israel, for he already had a son, Jonathan, who with his
father entered with heroism and daring upon their one
great task of conquering the Philistines. Early in Saul's
reign he became involved with David, the close friend of
his son, the husband of his daughter Michal, his own
armour-bearer, and a most able soldier, who because of his
strength and popularity fired the king with jealousy and
fear, and finally with suspicion and hatred. The story of this
suspicion and hatred is a sad and sorry one, for these pas-
sions either caused or increased actual illness in the mind
of Saul, an illness which resulted in inglorious and treacherous schemes for David's death and finally in Saul's own
suicide after a disastrous defeat at the hands of the Philistines. Jonathan was slain in the same lost battle.

David, who during Saul's enmity toward him had lived
as an outlaw in the wilderness, gathering around him all
manner of disgruntled and dissatisfied freebooters and even
pretending to ally himself with the Philistine king of Gath,
was quick to seize upon the chance afforded him by the
death of Saul. With the consent of the Philistines and even
perhaps as their vassal, he set up for himself a small prin-
cipality in the town of Hebron, an ancient religious center
south of Jerusalem (which was then only the stronghold of
a Canaanitish tribe known as the Jebusites), and held Hebron against the soldiers of Saul and against the king's weak
son, who had succeeded him. In the bitter struggle which

followed between the forces of Saul and those of David, David became increasingly the people's choice until around the year 1000 B.C. he became at the age of thirty-seven the second king of Israel.

The strong tribes of the north came to Hebron to make a covenant with this ruler from the southern tribe of Judah; and with the support now of all his kinsmen David moved on to strengthen his new kingdom. One of his first acts as king was to capture the strong Jebusite fortress of Jerusalem, helped by the genius of Joab, the captain of his army. This was a most wise and ingenious stroke, since Jerusalem was a completely neutral site, which had no earlier connection with any of the Israelite tribes. With Jerusalem as his capital city and royal seat, the loyalties of all Israel could be centered upon it and upon this sudden new order of political domination. To Jerusalem David, as sincere in his religious zeal as was Saul, though in no sense a pioneer in religious thought, like Moses, brought up the sacred Ark of the Covenant with song and pageantry, another act which forged strong religious ties between him and his people. And in his new city he built a palace for himself and for his wives and his concubines, after a luxurious fashion which would have seemed both distasteful and wrong to King Saul, his far more simple predecessor.

In spite of human weaknesses often seen in a personality so vivid and rich as was that of David, he was a great king over his people, and his importance in the history of Israel is immeasurable. He thoroughly defeated the Philistines who, after his victory over them, retired to their original cities and were never again a serious threat. They later even served in David's army as mercenaries! He brought under his dominion the remaining troublesome neighbours, such

as the Moabites, the Ammonites, and the Edomites. He
forced the Syrians to the north to pay him tribute money.
He entered into most diplomatic and valuable trade rela-
tions with Hiram, king of Tyre in Phoenicia. From a small
and negligible country, which had counted for nothing in
terms of wealth and prestige among the great kingdoms of
its time, he built up an actual empire, miniature perhaps in
comparison with the empires of Mesopotamia and Egypt,
but certainly the most important among the lesser powers
and the leading state between Egypt and Assyria.

This second king of Israel was a brilliant and shrewd
statesman, the ideal king of his grateful, united people; yet
in marked contrast to his political brilliance was his complete failure as a father of disloyal sons. The treacheries of
Amnon, Absalom, and Adonijah darkened and distressed
the last years of his life, as the vivid chapters in II Samuel
9–20, together with I Kings, chapters 1 and 2, bear honest,
realistic, and even ruthless witness. This so-called Court
History, written some years after David's death by a priest
of his household, a man probably named Ahimaaz, and the
most remarkable single historical narrative in the Old Testament, should be read by all who want to know just what
David was, both as a man and as a king.

In fairness to him, perhaps we should grant that few men,
whether kings or commoners, have had so candid and out-
spoken a biographer; and yet we must grant also that few
men have possessed so volatile and contradictory a nature.
We must remember, however, that he was, in point of fact,
an ancient king in an age still primitive and barbarous. He
was, according to the standards of his time, a great ruler,
more generous than most men and even to his enemies,
courageous and daring at any cost, ambitious for his coun-

try as well as for himself, capable of gaining and retaining
the almost incredible devotion of his soldiers, willing and
ready to acknowledge his own guilt and sin, and from first
to last passionately devoted to the God of Israel, whom he
served according to the customs and the dictates of his age.

As Moses had instilled the Hebrew tribes at Goshen and
in the wilderness with a sense of their identity as a people,
so David was in a very real sense the founder of the new
kingdom of Israel. Had his failure as a father not been so
marked and so fatal, had a son other than Solomon been
trained to take his place, the kingdom which he founded
might well have endured and prospered.

It has been truly said that Solomon is one of the most
over-rated men in history. Surely among all Old Testament
figures he has no equal for largely undeserved praise. The
pampered son of Bathsheba and David, he had inherited the
vices of his father without either his father's strength or vir-
tues. Skillfully promoted by his mother for the throne, he
acceded to it, as the Court History describes in I Kings 1,
with its awful candour, through the weakness and sensu-
ality of his dying father. Renowned for his wisdom, which
his unwise reign as the third and last king of a united Israel
surely does not substantiate; famous throughout Israel and
elsewhere for the luxury, splendour, and magnificence of
his court; lauded for the Temple which he built in Jerusalem to the God of Israel, toward whom, in spite of legends
extolling his religious zeal, he did not share the loyalty of
Saul and David; married to foreign wives who demanded of
him, and *got*, altars to their own strange gods;—he contributed lavishly more toward the disruption of Israel as a
kingdom than to its endurance and prosperity.

He was eager to deal commercially with the greater nations of his day, and to this end he encouraged all manner of costly enterprises, from the selling of horses in Egypt to digging mines for copper at Ezion-Geber on the Gulf of Aqabah. Archaeologists have discovered the many stables for his horses and cleverly designed smelting furnaces for his mines. He entered into treaty obligations with the port of Tyre by which he used Phoenician ships to market his goods and Phoenician architects and craftsmen to build not only his Temple, but his palace, luxurious homes for his many wives, and fortifications for the walls of Jerusalem and for other cities as well throughout his kingdom. Finally he became so deeply in debt to Hiram of Tyre that he was driven to give over to him twenty northern towns to discharge his obligations. Edom and Syria revolted against him, and by their revolt cost him not only territory, but the control of valuable trade routes.

A country so small as Israel could not pay the enormous costs of his ambitious building programs and of the supplies for his fabulous way of living. Taxes became unbearable, and the labour battalions which he drafted as he saw fit stirred up resentment early in his reign. He may have amazed and delighted the more prosperous and wealthy among his subjects; but the poor among them became steadily poorer and more discontented with their lot.

The tales of his wisdom and glory are surely dismally counteracted by the fears and sufferings of his oppressed citizenry and by the anger of other nations. Did the Queen of Sheba travel 1000 miles by caravan from her small kingdom in southern Arabia merely to look upon so wise a ruler and ask him questions? And were her reputed gifts of sandalwood, spices, precious stones, and a vast amount of money given only in homage to his wisdom and his glory?

Or, instead, might it not well be that she came in the interests of her own subjects and of her own land, which Solomon might well have been using at will for his commerce and trade? We read that Solomon gave her "all her desire, whatsoever she asked." Perhaps one of the things she asked was that he cease from making inroads into her domains!

The northern tribes of Israel, who had made a covenant with King David at Hebron, apparently suffered in particular from the abuse of King Solomon's power, for it was among them that rebellion finally arose. They might have been loyal to a king who needed support for some national crisis to which a whole people could respond; but they felt only hatred and distrust over his demands that by heavy taxation and forced labour they make possible his continued magnificence. Their growing dislike of him lay mainly in their recognition that the welfare of all his subjects was not his chief desire as it had been with Saul and with David. They could not blind their eyes to his despotism, his materialism, his lust for power, his weak concessions to his foreign wives, his favouritism toward the south. In the end it was they who rose against him.

4. The Age of the Two Kingdoms

The son of Solomon, Rehoboam, upon his accession to the throne of his father, was uneasily conscious that he had ten recalcitrant tribes in the northern part of his kingdom to deal with, indeed to mollify. Nor were they without a leader. A certain Jeroboam, who had been a discontented agitator among the labourers transported from the north by Solomon, rose to sponsor their cause after he had returned

from Egypt, where he had fled for asylum until Solomon's
death. Jeroboam may have had no right to rule over any
northern kingdom, which, seeing the bitterness of the people, he was quick to envisage; but he had strength and purpose, and surely a determination against Rehoboam and the
one strong southern tribe of Judah, only slightly increased
in numbers by the men of Benjamin.

The Old Testament tells us far too little about Rehoboam; but its sparse words, written in I Kings 12, can
leave no doubt in the mind of any reader that he was a dis-
dainful, arrogant, and most reckless young man. When, with
members of his court, he had journeyed north to Shechem,
an ancient, holy place since the days of the patriarchs, in the
hope of winning the support of his northern subjects, he
most stupidly decided to act upon the advice of his young
counsellors who had grown up with him rather than upon
that of the older advisers and statesmen of his father. The
older men, having listened to the complaints of the north,
counselled understanding and leniency; the younger men
advised harshness; and Rehoboam's fatal sense of new importance and power swayed him toward the unwise counsel
of his contemporaries. He may well have been the most
garrulous of princes; but history has recorded only a few
decisive and terrible words uttered by him. When his wait-
ing, sullen northern tribesmen asked him for a less grievous
yoke in return for their fealty, he replied:

"My father made your yoke heavy, and I will add to your
yoke. My father chastised you with whips, but I will chastise
you with scorpions!"

The response of the north was immediate and summary.
"What portion have we in David?" the men are said to have
cried. "To your tents, O Israel!" And though the now

frightened Rehoboam sent an ambassador to them in the
forlorn hope of a peaceful settlement, they stoned him to
death, and thereupon saw their former king flee southward
toward Jerusalem and his tribe of Judah. Jeroboam straight-
way became the first king of the northern kingdom.

It would be confusing and impossible in so short a sketch
as this to follow all events in these two small kingdoms. The
northern, that of Israel, lasted for two hundred years when
it was overthrown by Assyria in 722 B.C. The southern,
that of Judah, in spite of Assyrian inroads, managed to exist
until 598 B.C. when Nebuchadnezzar of Babylon, the successor to Assyrian might, despoiled Jerusalem and in 587
B.C. completed his conquest of Judah and his deportation
of its leading citizens. Good and evil rulers followed one
another in each kingdom, their goodness or their evil being
defined as to whether or not they had followed the faith of
Moses and of their fathers. The two books of Kings are
laconic enough, probably because longer chronicles of the
separate reigns had been given elsewhere, as is surely suggested by the repeated formula: *Now the rest of the acts of
—Jeroboam, or Hezekiah, or Ahab, or Uzziah—are they
not given in the Book of the Chronicles of the Kings of
Israel—or of Judah?* Today we know nothing of this Book,
surely not to be confused with the much later Biblical books
of that name. Apparently such an account once existed,
though it is now unfortunately lost.

Israel had her powerful rulers such as Omri, sometimes
called "the David of the North" and his son Ahab, neither
of whom, whatever his strength, can be said to have ad-
vanced the cause of the God of all the tribes, north and
south. Still they brought the northern peoples together in
political unity and gloried in their new capital city of

Samaria, which, they boasted, was a worthy counterpart to
Jerusalem. Judah under such kings as Asa, Hezekiah, and
Josiah, attempted religious reforms, for the worship of
strange gods was always a problem to both kingdoms.
Neither kingdom, in point of fact, in spite of promising periods under strong rulers, was able to build up any com-
manding political power. Their one frail hope had lain in
unity; and this was now lost. It was the strong *religious* distinction of the Hebrew peoples which marked them as
peculiarly gifted; and this religious distinction during these
centuries of schism was constantly imperilled from forces
both within and without. The divided monarchy, if one
appraises it quite truly, went constantly downward instead
of upward, as the Hebrew prophets from Elijah to Jeremiah understood all too well when they did their utmost to
bring it back to God.

Of far greater interest to the general reader and student
than a succession of kings are the differences which from
the beginning marked the two kingdoms and which were
in the end to prove the collapse and destruction of both.
The north, Israel, was from the start the stronger kingdom
both in terms of population and of the nature of its land. It
was largely an agricultural country with fields and vineyards, flourishing towns, streams, and relatively open, pro-
ductive acreage. Yet its very richness resulted in a prosperity which in turn brought about its own evils. Its neighbours, too, were anything but helpful, either in politics or in
religion, or, for that matter, in ethnic unity. Syria on the
north was strong and greedy; Phoenicia on the west made
alliances most costly; and far to the east the great and growing empire of Assyria was a terrifying menace, like some
fierce lion, its emblem, arousing himself and making ready

for a kill. There were constant infiltrations into a land so open, so lacking in natural defenses, of neighbouring aliens, all of whom brought their gods along with them. Northern kings, like Ahab, for diplomatic reasons made foreign marriages, which again meant foreign gods. There are few persons who do not know of Jezebel, the princess of Tyre whom Ahab married, her god Melkart, the "prophets" whom she imported, her theft of Naboth's vineyard, her terrible death at the hands of the fanatical Jehu, her head, hands, and feet, which even the dogs refused to eat. With all its wealth and independence the northern kingdom was doomed at the start, as the prophet Amos well knew when, some thirty years before its final ravaging by Assyria, he came striding from the wilderness of Tekoa into its shrine at Bethel to vent his rage against its wealth, its winter houses and its summer houses, its beds of ivory, its treatment of the poor, its drunkenness, its apostasy and idolatry.

Judah, the southern kingdom, was far more isolated among its hills than was Israel. It had one great advantage over the north: its relatively stable dynasty of David. But it was a small country, arid and barren for the most part, cut into dry valleys, the water supply for its cities and towns always a major problem. Farther from Assyria though it was, less open to attack than its northern neighbour, it had its own disadvantages which even the Holy City of Jerusalem and the name of David could not dispel. One of the chief drawbacks to its prosperity and progress was the loss of the most frequented and most valuable trade routes which wound through northern territory and which were, of course, strongly held by the north. Another was its greater nearness to less civilized peoples and to marauding tribes of the desert. Still another was the flourishing of polytheistic and pagan cults, lesser than in the north, but never absent, either from infiltration or from past Canaanitish loyalties, which had never completely vanished.

All in all, small kingdoms, no matter how ambitious, were clearly not framed to flourish in a time when great powers were once again rampant and rapacious. Judah lasted longer than Israel, to be sure, but only at the cost of paying a heavy tribute to Assyria, to whom the southern kingdom was, in fact, a vassal, and of allowing kings, like the evil Manasseh, to be sycophants to its empire over a period of many years.

When, in 722 B.C., Assyria gobbled up Israel, which had made a valiant, but futile alliance with Syria in order to withstand the Assyrian hosts, Sargon, the Assyrian emperor, transported thousands of northerners to Mesopotamia, being careful to take away the best of the people lest they might make further trouble at home. At the same time he brought possible Assyrian malcontents into Israel. From the inevitable mixture, as time went on, the Samaritans sprang, a mixed breed always scorned by the people of Judah and unpopular and suspected even centuries later in Jesus' day as the Gospels tell us,—and often to the credit of the despised Samaritans!

The deported Israelites from the north seem to have merged completely into their new home, so completely that they are sometimes called "the lost ten tribes of Israel." They early forsook any tribal entities and apparently made no attempt to preserve their identity. It was the people of Judah, later taken to Babylon, who were tenacious of both their nation and their religion. It was they who made possible for us our Hebraic-Christian inheritance, they who upon their Return assembled the Old Testament.

Perhaps the Hebrew prophets tell us more about the conditions existing in the two kingdoms than do any of the accounts in the books of Kings. To them we shall now turn.

5. The Age of the Prophets

The noble teachings of the great Hebrew prophets echo throughout the Psalms: the patience and mercy of God toward men; His demands for justice and uprightness in life; His nearness and His majestic distance, alike; His active participation in the affairs of men; His purposes in history; His yearning over His children; His desire, not for empty outward forms, but for a pure and contrite heart.

> *For I desired mercy and not sacrifice,*
> *And the knowledge of God more than burnt offerings,*

declares Hosea, the prophet of the northern kingdom, before its ravaging by Assyria. The author of Psalm 51 repeats his thought and many of his words when he writes:

For thou desirest not sacrifice, else would I give it;
Thou delightest not in burnt offerings.
The sacrifices of God are a broken spirit.
A broken and a contrite heart, O God, thou wilt not despise.

We often say that *prophecy* was a strictly Hebrew institution, that just as Greece produced her philosophers and Rome her statesmen, so Israel (which will be used from now on to denote a people and a nation rather than a northern kingdom) produced her prophets. This statement is not strictly true. Other peoples in the early, crude stages of prophecy had their prophets also. There were Canaanite prophets of Baal, and Amorite prophets, and prophets of Phoenicia. And yet they bore almost no resemblance to the distinctive Hebrew prophets, Amos, Hosea, Micah, Isaiah, and Jeremiah, who rose about 750 B.C. and who for 150 years concerned themselves with the religious and social conditions, and, in the case of Isaiah and of Jeremiah, the political affairs of their disrupted country. So, in a very real sense, prophecy in its highest form, *was* a Hebrew institution. This statement leads us, of course, to a consideration of the background and the forebears of those greatest Hebrew prophets, who revealed anew with astounding courage the demands of God, who concerned themselves with the affairs of men, and who were the forerunners of Jesus of Nazareth, Himself a prophet.

Prophecy in its earliest manifestations was exemplified by *bands* of prophets, who seem to have been groups of men given to religious frenzy and who went about the country stirring up religious enthusiasm and perhaps political as well. Such groups were probably most influential among the lower classes, who believed that they possessed miraculous powers. Between them and the true prophets a great gulf was fixed, as we realize when Amos declares to the priest at Bethel that he has no relationship to these professional agitators.

Another stage in Hebrew prophecy is exemplified by the speaking prophet Elijah and, to a lesser extent, by Elisha, who followed his great master. Elijah, as we read in the brilliant narratives of I Kings 17-21, was a powerful and terrifying influence during the reign of King Ahab in the ninth century B.C. Truly a servant of God in his outcries against the prophets of Baal, 450 of whom he is said to have slain, and against the wickedness of Jezebel and Ahab, he yet retained certain primitive beliefs, as is proved by his desperate journey south to the wilderness of Sinai where he obviously believed that the God of Israel still dwelt.

Nor should we forget that the term *prophet* was given to men who sometimes lived at the court of certain kings or at least were consulted by them. Nathan at the court of David was such a man, probably an adviser to the king. So was Ahijah, who warned Jeroboam of the result of his wicked deeds.

These men, however, just as were the bands of prophets, were quite different from those great teachers of Israel who lived during the years of the two kingdoms and whose task, first of all, was to reveal the true nature of the God of Israel and to bring home to their people the injustices and the evils, both social and religious, of their time. Yet in order to understand these great prophets in all their dignity and stature, it is necessary to rid our minds of certain common misconceptions concerning them.

They were *not* in any sense diviners or soothsayers; in fact, they scorned such absurd and superstitious clap-trap. They did *not* predict the future, an idea to many people inherent in the very word *prophet*. To their always realistic minds, the future was the inevitable result of the present. If men persisted in idolatry and in other forms of sin, then their future was bound to result in a falling away from God and, consequently, in suffering and tragedy.

They were *not* mere social reformers. Their thoughts were far higher than security and welfare, the rehabilitation of people, social and economic justice, the so-called "rights of man." To think of them only in this narrow sense is to misunderstand completely their great gifts to their country and, indeed, to all mankind. Instead, they saw the whole people of Israel so marked by a religious purpose and destiny that, by the Covenant made with God, they were

committed to acts of righteousness and justice in their daily
life. Since religion was the very core of their existence, they
thought, first of all, of a man's personal responsibility before
God. The demands of that responsibility must, to be sure,
result in communal obligations; but it was the *persistent, active inculcation* of religious meaning into *every aspect*, however small, of human life which was the basis of all their
teachings. This religious significance of all life must never
be forgotten in any study of their high purpose, for it lies
at the very root of Hebrew prophecy.

In spite of the quite natural desire of Christian apologists,
saints, and scholars, the Hebrew prophets did *not* span six
or seven long centuries and foresee the coming of Jesus of
Nazareth. It is a simple violation of historical truth to think
that they did so. The real truth lies in the recognition that
the prophets were in a line of religious growth and development which culminated in Jesus. He, as we have said, was
Himself a prophet, whose teachings and whose life on earth
revealed even more perfectly the deeply religious perceptions of the Hebrew prophets seven hundred years before
His day. If we see them as forecasters or foreseers of Him
(which they were *not*), we shall run the risk of not seeing
them as they were in their own time of violence and evil
when both the lives of nations and the guilty souls of men
were at stake. We shall fail, too, in understanding their own
wonderful conceptions of God, which for their age were
profound and remarkable and which were always to be
honoured and cherished in the history not only of their own
people, but of the world.

And now, having seen what they were *not*, what *were*
these greatest of the Hebrew prophets? They were, quite
simply, the spokesmen of God to His people. This they

devoutly believed they had been called to be, and this call
they acted upon. The heart of Hebrew prophecy is, then,
neither prediction nor social reform, but the declaration of
the Will of God for men.

The prophets were, as we have seen, deeply religious
men in the sense that their knowledge of God and their
experience with Him formed the impregnable center out of
which came their teaching. Nevertheless, they were *realists*.
They may have had what is often known as "mystic communion" with God; but to an astonishing degree their feet
were solidly placed upon the earth and their minds just as
firmly and uncompromisingly fixed upon their world. To
them a *vision*, which was frequently given to them, for they
were men of lofty dreams and visions, was in no sense un-
connected with idolatrous practices or with silly women
who drank too much or who wore too much jewelry.
Isaiah, for example, could be overcome by a beatific vision
of the Lord of hosts in the Temple at Jerusalem on one day,
and on the next advise a stupid king against a political alliance with his neighbours. He surely saw no incongruity in
the juxtaposition of these seemingly disparate events! Unless
we can see the prophets as unworldly, yet concerned with
the world, as angry, yet compassionate, as unyielding, yet
merciful, as despairing, yet filled with hope, as mystic, yet
realistic,—we shall fail to see them at all, and in that failure
learn little of what they meant to the backsliding, careless,
indulgent people of their time and place, which were the
time and place of the two kingdoms before their downfall.

We cannot here study all the five great Hebrew prophets
as individuals, engrossing though each of them is. Readers
who are interested in them will find in the reading list books
especially selected because they contain fascinating ac-

counts of them and of their work. Having tried to define them, I shall now attempt to explain the evils which they felt sure were corrupting their people and making their destruction sure and certain unless they returned to their God and to the terms of the Covenant made with Him five centuries earlier under the leadership of Moses.

Just as a profound religious consciousness lay behind and within every act of each of the prophets, so all united in the condemnation of the evils of their day. They condemned idolatry—the persistence of Canaanite "high places," the observance of sensual cults and customs, such as temple prostitution, the erection of altars to foreign gods, the performance of empty sacrificial rites, even to their own God— in short, the neglect of those vows and promises which their forefathers had made. And all are constantly proclaiming that it is not sacrifice which God demands, for sacrifice is irrelevant to the main concern of religion, but, rather, honesty and uprightness in life.

They all inveigh against social sins, the follies and extravagance of the rich, bribery, extortion, the treatment of the poor, who, Amos says, have been sold "for a pair of shoes." They inveigh, too, against luxury, which was especially characteristic of the north, where easy prosperity and long seasons of freedom from war had resulted in a crass materialism. Micah in the south, from a peasant village near Jerusalem, fears and condemns the arrogant, rich landholders and merchants who forget the command of God that men shall "do justly, love mercy, and walk humbly" with Him.

The women both of the north and of the south merit scathing diatribes. Amos likens them to cows, to the fat "kine of Bashan." They beg drink of their husbands; they oppress the poor and needy. Isaiah describes with awful irony the women of Jerusalem, their well-set hair, their nose jewels, their many changes of apparel, their mirrors, and their perfume. The day will come, he says, when they shall be bald and when their perfume will turn to *stink!* Their husbands and their sons, too, shall fall by the sword of the conquerors.

Perhaps the prophets are most angry, and sorrowful as well, when in the name of God they cry out against the prevalent apathy, carelessness, and indifference. To them all, this indifference is the unforgivable sin in the face of the mercy and tenderness of God. Hosea, in the heart-broken voice always characteristic of him, pleads with the people of the north to return to God in whom alone there is hope of redemption; and Jeremiah, writing more than a hundred years later in the south echoes Hosea's sadness as he tries to make the men and women of Judah realize that nearness to God and communion with Him means not only the fulfillment of a vow, but the only hope and safety for the human soul.

Yet none of the prophets is without hope. Relying on the immovable promises of God, all believe that a remnant of the nation will in the end be redeemed and saved. Sin must have its consequences; those who do wrong must pay, and perhaps a costly, tragic price. Nevertheless, since God is supreme in history, His purposes and promises alike sure and certain, the day of redemption though far off, far beyond their own bitter day, must dawn. It may come through the birth and the sovereignty of a just prince, who walks always in the ways of God; or it may come only as the result of grievous suffering and repentance when men once again see the light of truth.

This hope and faith Isaiah, perhaps the greatest of all the prophets, expresses in his stirring lines:

And there shall be a highway for the remnant of his people . . . like as it was to Israel in the day that he came up out of the land of Egypt. And in that day thou shalt say, O Lord, I will praise thee. Though thou wast angry with me, thine anger is turned away, and thou comfortedest me. I will trust and not be afraid; for the Lord God is my strength and my song. He also is become my salvation.

6. The Age of the Exile in Babylon

Exile is not a pleasant word; nor was it a pleasant fate for those Judeans who were taken away from home by Nebuchadnezzar in 598 B.C. and again in 587 after he had returned to despoil their Holy City and much of their country as well. Babylon, to be sure, was a beautiful city, the most beautiful of the ancient world. Its temples, palaces, and gardens were the wonder of their age. It lay, too, in a fertile river valley. Its land was neither arid nor barren nor swept by hot, searing winds as was Judea among its ragged, stony hills.

Nor, so far as history tells us, were the exiles treated badly in any way. They seem to have been allowed to live in their own agricultural colonies in the nearby countryside, to preserve their own customs, to follow, if they wished, their own religion. Before the close of their fifty years in Babylonia several had found their way into the great city itself and had entered into thriving commercial enterprises. The burden of their exile lay in other spheres than the physical, the social, or the economic.

Many of them, of course, decided to stay in Babylonia,

perhaps seeing no future in Judea, even when and *if* they should be allowed to return, perhaps thinking that this alien land was a better, easier place in which to live and to bring up their families. But there were others among them who each year felt the burden of exile heavier, less tolerable. These were they of Psalm 137, who "wept when they remembered Zion."

For the burden which the still faithful found unbearable was comprised of other griefs than those of mere absence from home. It contained the knowledge of guilt and failure, of indifference to the commands of God; the fear that God had not only justly punished, but deserted them; the awful dread that they would never again see their homeland; the terrible and terrifying thought that their life as a nation was ended. To such faithful, if desperate souls the ease and comparative freedom of existence in Babylonia was ironic instead of comforting, anxious instead of tranquil, full of care instead of careless.

Yet, as time went on, they were not without those who gave help and encouragement. Two names stand out brilliantly against this dark half-century of subjection and mental suffering: one, that of Ezekiel, who was not only a prophet, but, more important during this tragic time, a pastor to the exiles; the other, that of an incomparable poet, who, because his actual name has been lost and because his poems and prophecies as well are included in the book of Isaiah, is known as Isaiah of Babylon, or Second-Isaiah.

Ezekiel, whose dull and repetitious outpourings, trances, ecstasies, and visions mark him as fanatical, dogmatic, and intolerant, nevertheless was surely a most powerful figure during those years of captivity. He had probably gone down to Babylon in 598 with the first of the exiles. Completely dominated by zeal for the God of Israel and entirely assured of His justice toward His suffering people, Ezekiel strove to keep alive that faith which had made Israel a people and a nation. Without doubt he was more contributive to the later history of Israel than many more appealing leaders. For he insisted on religious practices even in exile; established rites and ceremonies in accordance with the Law, which he knew and revered; made definite plans for rebuilding the destroyed sanctuaries of Jerusalem and Judea; laid emphasis alike on the holiness of God and on the duties and obligations of His faithful servants;—in short, established within an alien land a congregation bound to the belief in its survival as a religious institution and power, whatever might be its political fate. Dedicated to the assurance of the restoration of his people, he gave to those exiles who were still loyal to their faith a new moral and religious responsibility, a new dignity, and a flaming purpose. His Old Testament book may be difficult and bewildering to read, as it most certainly is; yet he frees himself from its puzzling intricacies in a wonderful way when we realize his service to the Babylonian exiles and to the religion of Israel.

There could hardly be a more vivid contrast between any two contemporaries in history than between Ezekiel and the poet of the exile, Isaiah of Babylon. This young poet, who was also a prophet of good tidings and of a new life, went about among the exiles speaking and writing not about the observance of the Law, but about the love of God, and love not alone for Israel, but for all mankind. Isaiah of Babylon was, in fact, the first *complete* monotheist of Israel; and his superb poems on the nature of this one and only God, at their best perhaps in Isaiah 40 to 43, inclusive, should be read by everyone.

He had other comforting thoughts for his people. He taught them that suffering for sin means not only repentance, atonement, and redemption, but even an offering to God and, as such an offering, a positive and active good, both for themselves and for others. He assured them of their return home, giving countless images of the care of God for them during their long journey. And he saw their final deliverance from exile not merely as freedom from subjection, but as rescue from the tyranny of defeatism and hopelessness, as a new entrance into the promises and the purposes of God.

This Isaiah of Babylon opened ways of thought and of expression unimagined by any prophet or poet before his day. Except for the author of the book of Job and a few poets of the Psalms, he is the greatest poet of the Old Testament in his wealth of imagery, the singing, mounting quality of his verse, and in his capacity for stirring the deepest emotions, both in his far-off day and in our own. Many of the psalmists must have known his poetry, for in their own lines are countless echoes of his imagery and even of his words. And yet like his great predecessor, Isaiah of Jerusalem, he never forgot the plight of his people, their frustrations, their sense of failure. Ecstatic as is his poetry, its object is his own time and place, and its theme God's ultimate triumph over all the world through the awakened faith and confidence of this sad, struggling Israel by the waters of Babylon.

With all her greatness and power Babylon fell in 538 B.C. before the armies of Persia, which for some years preceding had herself been experiencing conquest under Cyrus, the king of Media, now become sovereign of a vast empire.

Historians through the centuries have called this Cyrus, king of Persia, "one of the most enlightened rulers the world has ever seen." He quite clearly was generous toward customs and cultures different from his own, tolerant and understanding. Isaiah of Babylon saw in him the hope of exiled Israel, calling him the "shepherd" and even the "anointed" of God.

One of his first acts upon his subjugation of Babylonia was to grant permission to the exiled Jews to return to their own land; and in 537 B.C. those who still longed for Jerusalem and Judea set forth on their long, 800-mile journey homeward.

7. The Age of Subjection to Foreign Powers

During fully two centuries after the Return a dark curtain drops between the history of Israel and those of us who would learn about it. There are almost no fully reliable records of those many years when Judea was a distant, unimportant province of the great Persian Empire. Our knowledge of this period of time must be culled mainly from those portions of the Old Testament which tell too little about it: the two books of Chronicles, never too dependable; those of Ezra and Nehemiah, written also by the Chronicler; and the works of the so-called post-exilic prophets, chief among whom were Haggai, Zechariah, Malachi, and Joel. These men apparently lived in Jerusalem or at least in Judea during the years after the Return; and, although their writings seem, and are, didactic, pedantic, and dull in comparison with those of the great prophets, they are most valuable in affording at least some information concerning those conditions which the disheartened homecomers had to meet and to cope with.

The life of the returned exiles surely did not fulfill the ecstatic hopes of Isaiah of Babylon! They came back to a barren land, depleted in agriculture, beset by plagues of locusts and other insects, burned by drought, isolated from the major trade routes. That they were poor is proved by the prophetic writings which tell of meager harvests, apparently urged by the people as an excuse for failing to rebuild the Temple until twenty years after their return. Nor did they make out too well with their neighbours, either with those who had remained in Judea during the years of exile, or the Samaritans to the north, either with the Edomites to the south or with the inevitable aliens who wandered in to make new homes. Intermarriage with people of non-Semitic blood distressed both them and their watchful prophets who inveighed against it.

Sympathetic as one must be with their dashed hopes and dreams, one easily gathers that they were arrogant and exclusive as well as fearful and wretched. This exclusiveness was apparently furthered by two men who, nevertheless, contributed much toward keeping alive and active their sorely tested religious faith. One was Nehemiah, who around 444 B.C. returned from the court of Persia where he is said to have been a "cupbearer" to the king, and who had heard there of the situation in Jerusalem. He was made governor of the colony in Judea, which he at once separated as a district apart from Samaria. He began immediately to rebuild the broken-down walls of Jerusalem and to enforce religious observances upon the tired, lethargic, and discouraged population. Another was Ezra, apparently a priest and scribe, who, coming to Jerusalem around 398 B.C. further solidified the community by insisting on the newly codified Law as the basis of Jewish life. Rigid and intolerant as these men doubtless were, their policies and practices together with their ardent religious zeal were responsible to a large extent for the arousing and for the continuance of the Mosaic and the prophetic faith. In the books named for them the Old Testament gives us wonderful pictures of Nehemiah's boundless energy on his new walls and of Ezra's reading of the sacred Law to the assembled people.

The Temple, the erection of which had been begun in 520 B.C., was completed four years later. It was in no sense the Temple of Solomon; but it nevertheless meant the center of Jewish life and worship. It meant, too, the lodestone to Jewish colonies now scattered throughout Asia Minor, Egypt, and the Mediterranean world. Those who lived far away probably never looked upon it, yet they knew it was there, as the tangible symbol of their ancient faith; those who lived near enough journeyed back to it, as we have seen, to celebrate the religious festivals which took place within its gates and walls.

In 333 B.C. the Persians succumbed to the world conquest of Alexander of Macedon, and Judea knew yet another overlord, surely less welcome than Cyrus and his successors; for Alexander brought a militant Greek culture, hateful to the devout Jewish mind because of its aesthetic and humanistic outlook on life and its insistence on the right of private judgment in matters of religion. After Alexander's early death in 323 B.C. the surveillance of this vast empire was entrusted to those who had become his trusted followers. Chief among these were the Ptolemies of Egypt and the Seleucids of Syria, who held Antioch as their chief city. The unimportant, tiny province of Judea was subject to them both in turn.

In this Hellenistic period, too, or at least for one hundred and thirty years of it, it is difficult to rest upon any completely dependable records. Under the Ptolemies, however, there seems to have been no really serious repression of Jewish customs or of religious faith, although always the adherents of that faith resented bitterly Hellenistic, or late-Greek, customs and the charm which its easier ways exerted over many Israelites. With the Syrian domination, for which we possess far better authority, tyranny became the order of the day, especially under a ruler known as Antiochus Epiphanes, who attempted to deprive his Judean subjects of their religious life and to force upon them observances unbearable to them. The conflict between those who had been won over to Hellenistic ways of life and thought and the staunch followers of the faith of Israel grew steadily more bitter until Jerusalem and all Judea became not only turbulent but rebellious.

This Antiochus seems to have been a genius at conceiving insults. In the year 168 B.C., determined to make an end of the religion of his angry subjects, he forbade the rite of circumcision, the observance of the Sabbath, and the services in the Temple. As a culminating audacity he erected in place of the Temple altar one to Olympian Zeus and rededicated the Temple to the Greek god. Similar altars were built throughout the towns and villages of Judea, and sacrifices were ordered to be performed upon the occasion of pagan festivals. Persecution, even to death, was the lot of those who continued to proclaim their loyalty to the faith of Israel.

The result of this madness was the Wars of the Maccabees, led by Judas Maccabeus, or Judas the Hammerer, of the devout Hasmonean family. In a series of incredible battles, carried on mostly by guerilla warfare of the most desperate sort by untrained and unequipped forces against the trained armies of a powerful ruler, these Maccabees accomplished more than had seemed possible. At first they fought for religious liberty; then for political freedom; and finally, in a quite unrealistic, yet praiseworthy dream, for the restoration of the kingdom of David. These wars lasted over a period of a hundred years, pursued by Hasmonean descendants. Their high point was reached in 140 B.C. when a Hasmonean named Simon was declared high priest as well as civil ruler over Judea. Had the later rebels and leaders only possessed the religious and moral fervour of the earlier Maccabees, even more might have been accomplished toward the re-establishment of Israel as an independent nation before the Roman Empire began to cast its mighty shadow over Asia Minor and the Mediterranean world.

Israel came again to an end as a political entity in 63 B.C. before the legions of Rome; yet there was no end to her ancient religious faith, which had been the basis of her national unity for twelve hundred years. That religion which had marked Israel as distinctive among all the peoples of history survived all conquerors and empires, mighty though they were. It lived on in Jerusalem, Judea, and Galilee and in the countless Jewish communities spreading constantly throughout the world from Babylon and Alexandria to Greece and Rome, each with its synagogue, its learned priests and scribes, its Law, and its rabbinical schools. St. Luke in the second chapter of the Acts of the Apostles wrote truly when he said that on the day of Pentecost there were at Jerusalem devout Jews, "out of every nation under heaven."

It was during these obscure, dark, and troublous centuries after the Return from Exile, during the Persian and the Alexandrian subjection of Judea, roughly from 500 to 200 B.C., that most of the book of Psalms was written. To understand why the psalmists described the whole range of their ancient faith from its primitive to its most exalted ideas is not difficult when we realize the desperate struggles of Israel to preserve that faith against apostasy and desecration, poverty and persecution. Nor is it difficult to understand their need of God, their clinging both to the Law and to prophetic truths and teachings, their fear and hatred of their enemies both within and without, their greater fear of their own weakness and failure. More than any other of the Old Testament books, compiled or composed during those awful years of struggle and despair, the Psalms portray most truly the resilience and the strength of the human soul, which, having seemingly lost all, still endures in the knowledge and the confidence that it has not lost, or ever can lose, its God.

A List of Recommended Books

I am listing here only books which I myself have found most interesting and valuable. All will be found rewarding and helpful to the general reader.

BOOKS OF GENERAL INTEREST

Harper's Bible Dictionary, by M. S. and J. L. Miller. Harper, 1952.
This amazing volume has but one drawback: it is so engrossing that it compels neglect of everything else!

A Light to the Nations, by Norman Gottwald. Harper, 1959.
This is the most valuable single book I know on the literature of the Old Testament and on the history and the religion of Israel. It is at once scholarly and fascinating. *Don't fail to read and study it!*

The Books of the Old Testament, by Robert H. Pfeiffer. Harper, 1957.
This is an abridgment of Professor Pfeiffer's definitive and invaluable *Introduction to the Old Testament*, published by Harper in 1941. Both books are absolutely first-class.

The Old Testament and Modern Study, edited by H. H. Rowley. Oxford, 1951. A paperback edition was issued by Oxford in 1961. This is a collection of essays by foremost Old Testament scholars. They are perhaps not *easy* reading, but they are uniformly excellent. Chapter VI deals with the Psalms. Chapter V deals with the Prophets.

God and History in the Old Testament, by Harvey H. Guthrie, Jr. The Seabury Press, 1960.
This is a completely delightful, thorough, and interesting presentation of the relation of God to the history of Israel.

The Hebrew Iliad, translated from the Hebrew by Robert H. Pfeiffer, with an introduction by William G. Pollard. Harper, 1957.
This is the famous Court History of David as given in II Samuel 9–20, I Kings 1–2, with certain other background material added. It is a distinguished translation and a most interesting book.

Everyday Life in Old Testament Times, by E. W. Heaton. Scribner's, 1955.
This is a necessary book for all who would know what daily life was like in ancient Israel. Canon Heaton has written it, he says in his Preface, largely for school and college students, for teachers, and for the general reader. It is admirably illustrated, and every page of it is engrossing.

The Old Testament Prophets, by E. W. Heaton. Penguin Books, 1958.
This inexpensive paperback gives a splendid account of the great prophets, their age, their teachings, their faith, and their distinctive characters as individuals.

The Relevance of the Prophets, by R. B. Y. Scott. Macmillan, 1944.
This is one of the best books ever written on the prophets and prophecy.

The Philistines, Their History and Civilization, by R. A. S. Macalister. British Academy, 1914.
This is an old book, but it is still the best one on the Philistines. I should not wish anyone to miss learning about these remarkable Aegean people.

The Dead Sea Scrolls, by Millar Burrows. Viking, 1955.

More about the Dead Sea Scrolls, by Millar Burrows. Viking, 1958.
I am including these books on the Dead Sea Scrolls because I have found them so completely enthralling that I can't bear anyone should miss them. They are the best of many books about this marvellous discovery.

BOOKS ON THE PSALMS

The Poetry of the Old Testament, by T. H. Robinson. Duckworth, 1947.
This book analyzes the best of Old Testament poetry. It contains an extended and valuable study of the Psalms.

The Psalms and Their Meaning for Today, by Samuel Terrien.
Bobbs Merrill, 1952.
Professor Terrien's book is thorough and original. The psalms
are studied as types and most carefully presented.

Thirty Psalmists, by Fleming James. Putnam, 1938.
This book by the late Professor Fleming James is enthusiastic and
individual. It takes upon itself the charm of one who knows and
loves his subject.

A Fresh Approach to the Psalms, by W. O. E. Oesterley. Macmillan, 1937.
This is perhaps, for the general reader, the very best book on
the Psalms. Its eager writing, its thoroughness, and its quite
amazing familiarity with its subject—all make it indispensable.

The Psalms, edited by D. C. Simpson. Oxford, 1926.
This book is comprised of lectures on the Psalms given at Oxford
University by distinguished scholars. It is especially enlightening
in its treatment of foreign influences upon them. It is not easy
reading, but it is top-notch.